# Getting Started with Kubernetes

Orchestrate and manage large-scale Docker deployments with Kubernetes to unlock greater control over your infrastructure and extend your containerization strategy

**Jonathan Baier**

BIRMINGHAM - MUMBAI

# Getting Started with Kubernetes

First published: December 2015

Production reference: 1151215

Published by Packt Publishing Ltd.
Livery Place
35 Livery Street
Birmingham B3 2PB, UK.

ISBN 978-1-78439-403-5

www.packtpub.com

# Credits

**Author**
Jonathan Baier

**Reviewer**
Giragadurai Vallirajan

**Commissioning Editor**
Dipika Gaonkar

**Acquisition Editor**
Indrajit A. Das

**Content Development Editor**
Pooja Mhapsekar

**Technical Editor**
Gaurav Suri

**Copy Editor**
Dipti Mankame

**Project Coordinator**
Francina Pinto

**Proofreader**
Safis Editing

**Indexer**
Priya Sane

**Graphics**
Kirk D'Penha

**Production Coordinator**
Shantanu N. Zagade

**Cover Work**
Shantanu N. Zagade

# About the Author

**Jonathan Baier** is a senior cloud architect living in Brooklyn, NY. He has had a passion for technology since an early age. When he was 14 years old, he was so interested in the family computer (an IBM PCjr) that he poured through the several hundred pages of BASIC and DOS manuals. Then, he taught himself to code a very poorly-written version of Tic-Tac-Toe. During his teen years, he started a computer support business. Since then, he has dabbled in entrepreneurship several times throughout his life. He now enjoys working for Cloud Technology Partners, a cloud-focused professional service and application development firm headquartered in Boston.

He has over a decade of experience delivering technology strategies and solutions for both public and private sector businesses of all sizes. He has a breadth of experience working with a wide variety of technologies and with stakeholders from all levels of management.

Working in the areas of architecture, containerization, and cloud security, he has created strategic roadmaps to guide and help mature the overall IT capabilities of various enterprises. Furthermore, he has helped organizations of various sizes build and implement their cloud strategy and solve the many challenges that arise when "designs on paper" meet reality.

# Acknowledgments

A tremendous thank you to my wonderful wife, Tomoko, and my playful son, Nikko. You both gave me incredible support and motivation during the writing process. There were many early morning, long weekend, and late night writing sessions that I could not have done without you both. Your smiles move mountains I could not on my own. You are my true north stars and my guiding light in the storm.

I'd also like to extend special thanks to all my colleagues and friends at Cloud Technology Partners, many of whom provided encouragement and support throughout the process. I'd especially like to thank Mike Kavis, David Linthicum, Alan Zall, Lisa Noon, and Charles Radi, who helped me make the book so much better with their efforts. I'd also like to thank the amazing CTP marketing team (Brad Young, Shannon Croy, and Nicole Givin) for making my work look great on the Web and in front of the camera.

# About the Reviewer

**Giragadurai Vallirajan** is a seasoned technologist and entrepreneur. Currently, he is the CTO of Bluemeric Technologies Pvt Ltd, Bangalore. He has more than 12 years of experience in the IT industry and has worked for Fortune 100 companies, including Lehman Brothers (Tokyo) and Hewlett-Packard (Bangalore). Giragadurai has considerable expertise in big data analytics, predictive analytics, complex event processing, and performance tuning in distributed and cloud environments. He is an entrepreneur at heart; he started an analytics start-up, Vorthy Softwares (Singapore/ India), before joining Bluemeric.

# www.PacktPub.com

## Support files, eBooks, discount offers, and more

For support files and downloads related to your book, please visit www.PacktPub.com.

Did you know that Packt offers eBook versions of every book published, with PDF and ePub files available? You can upgrade to the eBook version at www.PacktPub.com and as a print book customer, you are entitled to a discount on the eBook copy. Get in touch with us at service@packtpub.com for more details.

At www.PacktPub.com, you can also read a collection of free technical articles, sign up for a range of free newsletters and receive exclusive discounts and offers on Packt books and eBooks.

https://www2.packtpub.com/books/subscription/packtlib

Do you need instant solutions to your IT questions? PacktLib is Packt's online digital book library. Here, you can search, access, and read Packt's entire library of books.

## Why subscribe?

- Fully searchable across every book published by Packt
- Copy and paste, print, and bookmark content
- On demand and accessible via a web browser

## Free access for Packt account holders

If you have an account with Packt at www.PacktPub.com, you can use this to access PacktLib today and view 9 entirely free books. Simply use your login credentials for immediate access.

# Table of Contents

# Preface

This book is a guide to getting started with Kubernetes and overall container management. We will walk you through the features and functions of Kubernetes and show how it fits into an overall operations strategy. You'll learn what hurdles lurk in moving container off the developer's laptop and managing them at a larger scale. You'll also see how Kubernetes is the perfect tool to help you face these challenges with confidence.

## What this book covers

*Chapter 1*, *Kubernetes and Container Operations*, provides a brief overview of containers and the how, what, and why of Kubernetes orchestration. It explores how it impacts your business goals and everyday operations.

*Chapter 2*, *Kubernetes – Core Concepts and Constructs*, will explore core Kubernetes constructs, such as pods, services, replication controllers, and labels using a few simple examples. Basic operations, including health checks and scheduling, will also be covered.

*Chapter 3*, *Core Concepts – Networking, Storage, and Advanced Services*, covers cluster networking for Kubernetes and the Kubernetes proxy, a deeper dive into services, storage concerns, persistent data across pods, and the container lifecycles. Finishing up, we will see a brief overview of some higher level isolation features for mutlitenancy.

*Chapter 4*, *Updates and Gradual Rollouts*, takes a quick look at how to roll out updates and new features with minimal disruption to uptime. We will also look at scaling the Kubernetes cluster.

*Chapter 5*, *Continuous Delivery*, will cover integration of Kubernetes into your continuous delivery pipeline. We will see how to use a K8s cluster with Gulp.js and Jenkins as well.

*Chapter 6, Monitoring and Logging,* teaches you how to use and customize built-in and third-party monitoring tools on your Kubernetes cluster. We will look at built-in logging and monitoring, the Google Cloud Logging service, and Sysdig.

*Chapter 7, OCI, CNCF, CoreOS, and Tectonic,* discovers how open standards benefit the entire container ecosystem. We'll look at a few of the prominent standards organizations and cover CoreOS and Tectonic. Also, we will explore their advantages as a host OS and enterprise platform.

*Chapter 8, Towards Production-Ready,* shows some of the helpful tools and third-party projects available and where you can go to get more help.

# What you need for this book

This book will cover downloading and running the Kubernetes project. You'll need access to a Linux system (VirtualBox will work if you are on windows) and some familiarity with the command shell.

In addition, you should have at least a Google Cloud Platform account. You can sign up for a free trial here:

`https://cloud.google.com/`

Also, an AWS account is necessary for a few sections of the book. You can also sign up for a free trial here:

`https://aws.amazon.com/`

# Who this book is for

Although you're in heads down in development, neck deep in operations, or looking forward as an executive, Kubernetes and this book are for you. *Getting Started with Kubernetes* will help you understand how to move your container applications into production with best practices and step-by-step walk-throughs tied to a real-world operational strategy. You'll learn how Kubernetes fits into your everyday operations and can help you prepare for production-ready container application stacks.

It will be helpful to have some familiarity with Docker containers, general software developments, and operations at a high level.

# Conventions

In this book, you will find a number of text styles that distinguish between different kinds of information. Here are some examples of these styles and an explanation of their meaning.

Code words in text, folder names, filenames, file extensions, and pathnames are shown as follows: "You can also use the `scale` command to reduce the number of replicas."

URLs are shown as follows:

```
https://docs.docker.com/installation/
```

If we wish you to use a URL after replacing a portion of it with your own values, it will be shown like this:

```
https://<your master ip>/swagger-ui/
```

Resource definition files and other code blocks are set as follows:

```
apiVersion: v1
kind: Pod
metadata:
  name: node-js-pod
spec:
  containers:
  - name: node-js-pod
    image: bitnami/apache:latest
    ports:
    - containerPort: 80
```

When we wish you to replace a portion of the listing with your own value, the relevant lines or items are set in bold between less than and greater than symbols:

```
subsets:
- addresses:
  - IP: <X.X.X.X>
  ports:
    - name: http
      port: 80
      protocol: TCP
```

Any command-line input or output is written as follows:

```
$ kubectl get pods
```

**New terms** and **important words** are shown in bold. Words that you see on the screen, for example, in menus or dialog boxes, appear in the text like this: "We can modify this group by clicking the **Edit group** button at the top of the page."

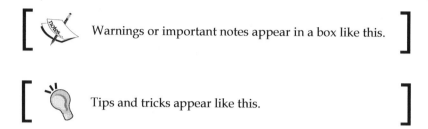

Warnings or important notes appear in a box like this.

Tips and tricks appear like this.

# Reader feedback

Feedback from our readers is always welcome. Let us know what you think about this book—what you liked or disliked. Reader feedback is important for us as it helps us develop titles that you will really get the most out of.

To send us general feedback, simply e-mail feedback@packtpub.com, and mention the book's title in the subject of your message.

If there is a topic that you have expertise in and you are interested in either writing or contributing to a book, see our author guide at www.packtpub.com/authors.

# Customer support

Now that you are the proud owner of a Packt book, we have a number of things to help you to get the most from your purchase.

# Downloading the example code

You can download the example code files from your account at http://www.packtpub.com for all the Packt Publishing books you have purchased. If you purchased this book elsewhere, you can visit http://www.packtpub.com/support and register to have the files e-mailed directly to you.

# Errata

Although we have taken every care to ensure the accuracy of our content, mistakes do happen. If you find a mistake in one of our books—maybe a mistake in the text or the code—we would be grateful if you could report this to us. By doing so, you can save other readers from frustration and help us improve subsequent versions of this book. If you find any errata, please report them by visiting http://www.packtpub.com/submit-errata, selecting your book, clicking on the **Errata Submission Form** link, and entering the details of your errata. Once your errata are verified, your submission will be accepted and the errata will be uploaded to our website or added to any list of existing errata under the Errata section of that title.

To view the previously submitted errata, go to https://www.packtpub.com/books/content/support and enter the name of the book in the search field. The required information will appear under the **Errata** section.

# Piracy

Piracy of copyrighted material on the Internet is an ongoing problem across all media. At Packt, we take the protection of our copyright and licenses very seriously. If you come across any illegal copies of our works in any form on the Internet, please provide us with the location address or website name immediately so that we can pursue a remedy.

Please contact us at copyright@packtpub.com with a link to the suspected pirated material.

We appreciate your help in protecting our authors and our ability to bring you valuable content.

# Questions

If you have a problem with any aspect of this book, you can contact us at questions@packtpub.com, and we will do our best to address the problem.

# 1
# Kubernetes and Container Operations

This chapter will give a brief overview of containers and how they work as well as why management and orchestration is important to your business and/or project team. The chapter will also give a brief overview of how **Kubernetes** orchestration can enhance our container management strategy and how we can get a basic Kubernetes cluster up, running, and ready for container deployments.

This chapter will include the following topics:

- Introducing container operations and management
- Why container management is important
- Advantages of Kubernetes
- Downloading the latest Kubernetes
- Installing and starting up a new Kubernetes cluster

## A brief overview of containers

Over the past two years, **containers** have grown in popularity like wildfire. You would be hard-pressed to attend an IT conference without finding popular sessions on Docker or containers in general.

Docker lies at the heart of the mass adoption and the excitement in the container space. As Malcom Mclean revolutionized the physical shipping world in 1957 by creating a standardized shipping container, which is used today for everything from ice cube trays to automobiles[1], Linux containers are revolutionizing the software development world by making application environments portable and consistent across the infrastructure landscape. As an organization, Docker has taken the existing container technology to a new level by making it easy to implement and ...

## WI

At th... ...d namespaces. Additionally, Docker uses ... ...ntainer development process.

**Con...** ...ost to share and also limit the ... ne. This is important for both, reso... **nial-of-service attacks** on the host ... share CPU and memory while stay...

Nan... ...way of processes. Processes are limi... ...nespace. Namespaces from other syst... ...container process. For example, a netv... ...etwork interfaces and configuration, whi... ..., routes, and firewall rules.

*[Handwritten notes:]*

*Kubernetes - mgmt & Orchestration*

*Docker - Core of container tech is about cgroups & namespaces*

*Cgroup - Allows the host to share & limit resources each process/container consumes. This avoids DDos, increased utilization. Several containers can share CPU within a predefined limit / constraints*

*Namespace - Allows isolation so processes are limited to see only those in that namespace*

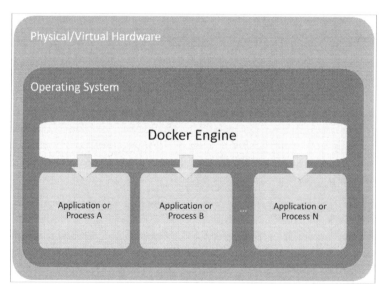

Figure 1.1. Composition of a container

**Union file systems** are also a key advantage to using Docker containers. The easiest ~~way to understand union file systems is to~~ think of them like a layer cake with each ~~layer... the kernel is our~~ el is our base layer; then, we might add ~~... Then,~~ we might add an application like **Nginx** ~~on top of each oth~~er. Finally, as you make changes and ~~... the final~~ top layer (think frosting) that is a

*[Handwritten note: Union file system — It is kind of layers with top most layer writable]*

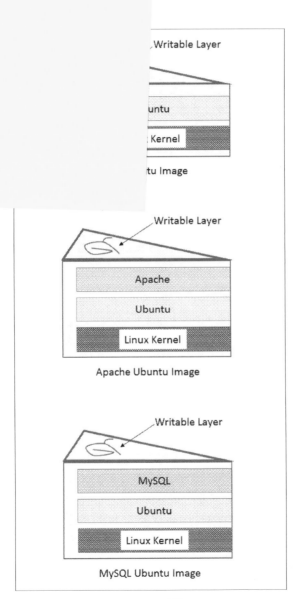

Figure 1.2. Layered file system

What makes this truly efficient is that Docker caches the layers the first time we build them. So, let's say that we have an image with Ubuntu and then add Apache and build the image. Next, we build MySQL with Ubuntu as the base. The second build will be much faster because the Ubuntu layer is already cached. Essentially, our chocolate and vanilla layers, from Figure 1.2, are already baked. We simply need to bake the pistachio (MySQL) layer, assemble, and add the icing (writable layer).

# Why are containers so cool?

Containers on their own are not a new technology and have in fact been around for many years. What truly sets Docker apart is the tooling and ease of use they have brought to community.

# Advantages to Continuous Integration/ Continuous Deployment

Wikipedia defines **Continuous Integration** as "the practice, in software engineering, of merging all developer working copies to a shared mainline several times a day." By having a continuous process of building and deploying code organizations are able to instill quality control and testing as part of the everyday work cycle. The result is that updates and bug fixes happen much faster and overall quality improves.

However, there has always been a challenge in setting development environments to match that of testing and production. Often inconsistencies in these environments make it difficult to gain the full advantage of continuous delivery.

Using Docker, developers are now able to have truly portable deployments. Containers that are deployed on a developer's laptop are easily deployed on an in-house staging server. They are then easily transferred to the production server running in the cloud. This is because Docker builds containers up with build files that specify parent layers. One advantage of this is that it becomes very easy to ensure OS, package, and application versions are the same across development, staging, and production environments.

Because all the dependencies are packaged into the layer, the same host server can have multiple containers running a variety of OS or package versions. Further, we can have various languages and frameworks on the same host server without the typical dependency clashes we would get in a **Virtual Machine** (**VM**) with a single operating system.

# Resource utilization

The well-defined isolation and layer filesystem also make containers ideal for running systems with a very small footprint and domain-specific purposes. A streamlined deployment and release process means we can deploy quickly and often. As such, many companies have reduced their deployment time from weeks or months to days and hours in some cases. This development life cycle lends itself extremely well to small, targeted teams working on small chunks of a larger application.

# Microservices and orchestration

As we break down an application into very specific domains, we need a uniform way to communicate between all the various pieces and domains. Web services have served this purpose for years, but the added isolation and granular focus that containers bring have paved a way for what is being named **microservices**.

The definition for microservices can be a bit nebulous, but a definition from Martin Fowler, a respected author and speaker on software development, says[2]:

> *"In short, the microservice architectural style is an approach to developing a single application as a suite of small services, each running in its own process and communicating with lightweight mechanisms, often an HTTP resource API. These services are built around business capabilities and independently deployable by fully automated deployment machinery. There is a bare minimum of centralized management of these services, which may be written in different programming languages and use different data storage technologies."*

As the pivot to containerization and microservices evolves in an organization, they will soon need a strategy to maintain many containers and microservices. Some organizations will have hundreds or even thousands of containers running in the years ahead.

# Future challenges

Life cycle processes alone are an important piece of operations and management. How will we automatically recover when a container fails? Which upstream services are affected by such an outage? How will we patch our applications with minimal downtime? How will we scale up our containers and services as our traffic grows?

Networking and processing are also important concerns. Some processes are part of the same service and may benefit from proximity on the network. Databases, for example, may send large amounts of data to a particular microservice for processing. How will we place containers *near* each other in our cluster? Is there common data that needs to be accessed? How will new services be discovered and made available to other systems?

Resource utilization is also a key. The small footprint of containers means that we can optimize our infrastructure for greater utilization. Extending the savings started in the elastic cloud world even further towards minimizing wasted hardware. How will we schedule workloads most efficiently? How will we ensure that our important applications always have the resources? How can we run less important workloads on spare capacity?

Finally, portability is a key factor in moving many organizations to containerization. Docker makes it very easy to deploy a standard container across various operating systems, cloud providers, and on-premise hardware, or even developer laptops. However, we still need tooling to move containers around. How will we move containers between different nodes on our cluster? How will we roll out updates with minimal disruption? What process do we use to perform blue-green deployments or canary releases?

Whether you are starting to build out individual microservices and separating concerns into isolated containers or if you simply want to take full advantage of the portability and immutability in your application development, the need for management and orchestration becomes clear.

# Advantages of Kubernetes

This is where orchestration tools such as Kubernetes offer the biggest value. **Kubernetes (K8s)** is an open source project that was released by Google in June, 2014. Google released the project as part of an effort to share their own infrastructure and technology advantage with the community at large.

Google launches 2 billion containers a week in their infrastructure and has been using container technology for over a decade. Originally they were building a system named **Borg**, and now **Omega**, to schedule their vast quantities of workloads across their ever-expanding data center footprint. They took many of the lessons they learned over the years and rewrote their existing data center management tool for wide adoption by the rest of the world. The result was the Kubernetes open source project[3].

Since its initial release in 2014, K8s has undergone rapid development with contributions all across the open source community, including Red Hat, VMware, and Canonical. The 1.0 release of Kubernetes went live in July, 2015. We'll be covering version 1.0 throughout the book. K8s gives organizations a tool to deal with some of the major operations and management concerns. We will explore how Kubernetes helps deal with resource utilization, high availability, updates, patching, networking, service discovery, monitoring, and logging.

# Our first cluster

Kubernetes is supported on a variety of platforms and OSes. For the examples in this book, I used an Ubuntu 14.04 Linux VirtualBox for my client and **Google Compute Engine (GCE)** with Debian for the cluster itself. We will also take a brief look at a cluster running on **Amazon Web Services (AWS)** with Ubuntu.

Most of the concepts and examples in this book should work on any installation of a Kubernetes cluster. To get more information on other platform setups, check the Kubernetes getting started page on the following GitHub link:

https://github.com/GoogleCloudPlatform/kubernetes/blob/v1.0.0/docs/getting-started-guides/README.md

First, let's make sure that our environment is properly set up before we install Kubernetes.

Start by updating packages:

```
$ sudo apt-get update
```

Install Python and curl if they are not present:

```
$ sudo apt-get install python
$ sudo apt-get install curl
```

Install the **gcloud** SDK:

```
$ curl https://sdk.cloud.google.com | bash
```

We will need to start a new shell before gcloud is on our path.

Configure your **Google Cloud Platform (GCP)** account information. This should automatically open a browser where we can log in to our Google Cloud account and authorize the SDK:

```
$ gcloud auth login
```

> If you have problems with login or want to use another browser, you can optionally use the `--no-launch-browser` command. Copy and paste the URL to the machine and/or browser of your choice. Log in with your Google Cloud credentials and click on **Allow** on the permissions page. Finally, you should receive an authorization code that you can copy and paste back into the shell where the prompt is waiting.

A default project should be set, but we can check this with the following:

```
$ gcloud config list project
```

We can modify this and set a new default project with this command. Make sure to use *project ID* and not *project name*, as follows:

```
$ gcloud config set project <PROJECT ID>
```

> We can find our project ID in the console at:
> `https://console.developers.google.com/project`
> Alternatively, we can list active projects:
> ```
> $ gcloud alpha projects list
> ```

Now that we have our environment set up, installing the latest Kubernetes version is done in a single step as follows:

```
$ curl -sS https://get.k8s.io | bash
```

It may take a minute or two to download Kubernetes depending on your connection speed. After this, it will automatically call the `kube-up.sh` script and start building our cluster. By default, it will use the Google Cloud and GCE.

> If something fails during the cluster setup and you need to start again, you can simply run the `kube-up.sh` script. Go to the folder where you ran the previous `curl` command. Then, you can kick off the cluster build with the following command:
> ```
> $ kubernetes/cluster/kube-up.sh
> ```

After Kubernetes is downloaded and the `kube-up.sh` script has started, we will see quite a few lines roll past. Let's take a look at them one section at a time.

```
Starting cluster using provider: gce
... calling verify-prereqs
WARNING: Component [preview] no longer exists.

All components are up to date.

All components are up to date.

All components are up to date.
```

Figure 1.3. GCE prerequisite check

 If your `gcloud` components are not up to date, you may be prompted to update.

The preceding section (Figure 1.3) shows the checks for prerequisites as well as makes sure that all components are up to date. This is specific to each provider. In the case of GCE, it will check that the SDK is installed and that all components are up to date. If not, you will see a prompt at this point to install or update.

```
... calling kube-up
Project: planaer-lear-758
Zone: us-central1-b
Creating gs://kubernetes-staging-3f2e2bfa6e
Creating gs://kubernetes-staging-3f2e2bfa6e/...
+++ Staging server tars to Google Storage: gs://kubernetes-staging-3f2e2bfa6e/de
vel
+++ kubernetes-server-linux-amd64.tar.gz already staged ('rm ./cluster/../cluste
r/gce/../../cluster/../server/kubernetes-server-linux-amd64.tar.gz.sha1' to forc
e)
+++ kubernetes-salt.tar.gz already staged ('rm ./cluster/../cluster/gce/../../cl
uster/../server/kubernetes-salt.tar.gz.sha1' to force)
```

Figure 1.4. Upload cluster packages

Now the script is turning up the cluster. Again, this is specific to the provider. For GCE, it first checks to make sure that the SDK is configured for a default **project** and **zone**. If they are set, you'll see those in the output.

Next, it uploads the server binaries to Google Cloud storage, as seen in the **Creating gs:\\...** lines.

```
Looking for already existing resources
Starting master and configuring firewalls
Created [https://www.googleapis.com/compute/v1/projects/planaer-lear-758/zones/us-central1-b/disks/kubernetes-master-pd].
NAME                  ZONE           SIZE_GB TYPE    STATUS
kubernetes-master-pd us-central1-b 20        pd-ssd READY
Created [https://www.googleapis.com/compute/v1/projects/planaer-lear-758/global/firewalls/kubernetes-master-https].
NAME                    NETWORK SRC_RANGES RULES    SRC_TAGS TARGET_TAGS
kubernetes-master-https default 0.0.0.0/0 tcp:443           kubernetes-master
Created [https://www.googleapis.com/compute/v1/projects/planaer-lear-758/regions/us-central1/addresses/kubernetes-master-
ip].
+++ Logging using Fluentd to gcp
Created [https://www.googleapis.com/compute/v1/projects/planaer-lear-758/global/firewalls/kubernetes-minion-all].
NAME                  NETWORK SRC_RANGES     RULES              SRC_TAGS TARGET_TAGS
kubernetes-minion-all default 10.244.0.0/16 tcp,udp,icmp,esp,ah,sctp      kubernetes-minion
Created [https://www.googleapis.com/compute/v1/projects/planaer-lear-758/zones/us-central1-b/instances/kubernetes-master]

NAME              ZONE          MACHINE_TYPE  PREEMPTIBLE INTERNAL_IP EXTERNAL_IP    STATUS
kubernetes-master us-central1-b n1-standard-1             10.240.0.2  107.178.208.84 RUNNING
```

Figure 1.5. Master creation

It then checks for any pieces of a cluster already running. Then, we finally start creating the cluster. In the output in Figure 1.5, we see it creating the **master** server, IP address, and appropriate firewall configurations for the cluster.

```
Creating minions.
Attempt 1 to create kubernetes-minion-template
WARNING: You have selected a disk size of under [200GB]. This may result in poor I/O performance. For more information, se
e: https://developers.google.com/compute/docs/disks/persistent-disks#pdperformance.
Created [https://www.googleapis.com/compute/v1/projects/planaer-lear-758/global/instanceTemplates/kubernetes-minion-templ
ate].
NAME                     MACHINE_TYPE  PREEMPTIBLE CREATION_TIMESTAMP
kubernetes-minion-template n1-standard-1             2015-10-10T09:34:43.734-07:00
Created [https://www.googleapis.com/compute/v1/projects/planaer-lear-758/zones/us-central1-b/instanceGroupManagers/kubern
etes-minion-group].
NAME                     ZONE          BASE_INSTANCE_NAME SIZE TARGET_SIZE GROUP                   INSTANCE_TEMPLATE
  AUTOSCALED
kubernetes-minion-group us-central1-b kubernetes-minion       4           kubernetes-minion-group kubernetes-minion-templa
te
Waiting for group to become stable, current operations: creating: 4
Waiting for group to become stable, current operations: creating: 4
Waiting for group to become stable, current operations: creating: 4
Waiting for group to become stable, current operations: creating: 3
Group is stable
MINION_NAMES=kubernetes-minion-9wqB kubernetes-minion-p0nf kubernetes-minion-vjwq kubernetes-minion-xysg
```

Figure 1.6. Minion creation

Finally, it creates the **minions** or **nodes** for our cluster. This is where our container workloads will actually run. It will continually loop and wait while all the minions start up. By default, the cluster will have four node (minions), but K8s supports having upwards of 100 (and soon beyond 1000). We will come back to scaling the nodes later on in the book.

```
Using master: kubernetes-master (external IP: 146.148.61.62)
Waiting for cluster initialization.

  This will continually check to see if the API for kubernetes is reachable.
  This might loop forever if there was some uncaught error during start
  up.

....................Kubernetes cluster created.
Wrote config for planaer-lear-758_kubernetes to /home/k8s/.kube/config

Kubernetes cluster is running.  The master is running at:

  https://146.148.61.62

The user name and password to use is located in /home/k8s/.kube/config.
```

Figure 1.7. Cluster completion

Now that everything is created, the cluster is initialized and started. Assuming that everything goes well, we will get an IP address for the master. Also, note that configuration along with the cluster management credentials are stored in home/**<Username>**/.kube/config.

```
... calling validate-cluster
Waiting for 4 ready nodes. 0 ready nodes, 2 registered. Retrying.
Waiting for 4 ready nodes. 0 ready nodes, 4 registered. Retrying.
Found 4 nodes.
      NAME                        LABELS                                              STATUS
    1 kubernetes-minion-ek3u      kubernetes.io/hostname=kubernetes-minion-ek3u       Ready
    2 kubernetes-minion-ppf6      kubernetes.io/hostname=kubernetes-minion-ppf6       Ready
    3 kubernetes-minion-sypt      kubernetes.io/hostname=kubernetes-minion-sypt       Ready
    4 kubernetes-minion-zr8g      kubernetes.io/hostname=kubernetes-minion-zr8g       Ready
Validate output:
NAME                  STATUS    MESSAGE              ERROR
controller-manager    Healthy   ok                   nil
scheduler             Healthy   ok                   nil
etcd-0                Healthy   {"health": "true"}   nil
Cluster validation succeeded
```

Figure 1.8. Cluster validation

Then, the script will validate the cluster. At this point, we are no longer running provider-specific code. The validation script will query the cluster via the kubectl. sh script. This is the central script for managing our cluster. In this case, it checks the number of minions found, registered, and in a ready state. It loops through giving the cluster up to 10 minutes to finish initialization.

After a successful startup, a summary of the minions and the cluster component health is printed to the screen:

```
Done, listing cluster services:

Kubernetes master is running at https://146.148.61.62
KubeDNS is running at https://146.148.61.62/api/v1/proxy/namespaces/kube-system/services/kube-dns
KubeUI is running at https://146.148.61.62/api/v1/proxy/namespaces/kube-system/services/kube-ui
Grafana is running at https://146.148.61.62/api/v1/proxy/namespaces/kube-system/services/monitoring-grafana
Heapster is running at https://146.148.61.62/api/v1/proxy/namespaces/kube-system/services/monitoring-heapster
InfluxDB is running at https://146.148.61.62/api/v1/proxy/namespaces/kube-system/services/monitoring-influxdb

Kubernetes binaries at /home/k8s/kubernetes/cluster/
You may want to add this directory to your PATH in $HOME/.profile
Installation successful!
```

Figure 1.9. Cluster summary

Finally, a `kubectl cluster-info` command is run, which outputs the URL for the master services as well as DNS, UI, and monitoring. Let's take a look at some of these components.

# Kubernetes UI

Open a browser and try the following code:

```
https://<your master ip>/api/v1/proxy/namespaces/kube-system/
services/kube-ui
```

The certificate is self-signed by default, so you'll need to ignore the warnings in your browser before proceeding. After this, we will see a login dialog. This is where we use the credentials listed during the K8s installation. We can find them at any time by simply using the `config` command:

```
$ kubectl config view
```

Now that we have credentials for login, use those, and we should see a dashboard like the following image:

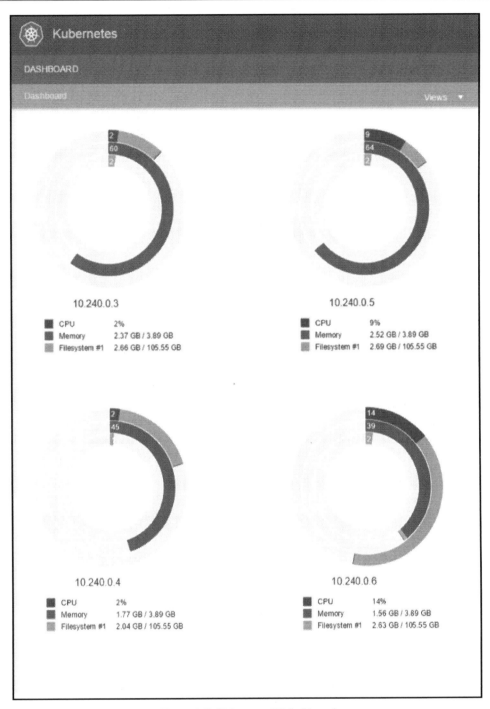

Figure 1.10. Kubernetes UI dashboard

The main dashboard page gives us a summary of the minions (or slave nodes). We can also see the CPU, memory, and used disk space on each minion as well the IP address.

The UI has a number of built-in views listed under the **Views** dropdown menu on the top right of the screen. However, most of them will be empty by default. Once workloads and services are spun up, these views will become a lot more interesting.

# Grafana

Another service installed by default is **Grafana**. This tool will give us a dashboard to view metrics on the cluster nodes. We can access it by using the following syntax in a browser:

```
https://<your master ip>/api/v1/proxy/namespaces/kube-system/
services/monitoring-grafana
```

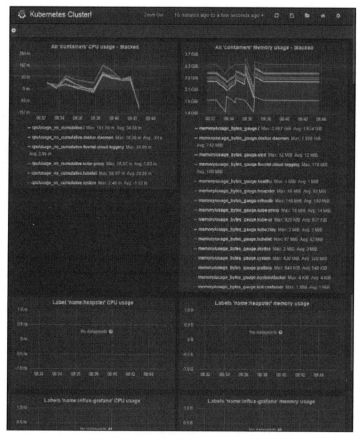

Figure 1.11. Kubernetes Grafana dashboard

Here, Kubernetes is actually running a number of services. **Heapster** is used to collect resource usage on the **pods** and **nodes** and stores the information in **InfluxDB**. The results, like CPU and memory usage, are what we see in the Grafana UI. We will explore this in depth in *Chapter 6, Monitoring and Logging*.

# Swagger

**Swagger** (`http://swagger.io/`) is a tool to add a higher level of interaction and easy discovery to an API.

Kubernetes has built a Swagger-enabled API, which can be accessed by using `https://<your master ip>/swagger-ui/`.

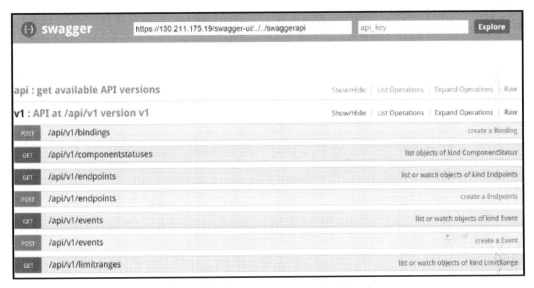

Figure 1.12. Kubernetes Swagger dashboard

Through this interface, you can learn a lot about the Kubernetes RESTful API. The bulk of the interesting endpoints are listed under `v1`. If we look at `/api/v1/nodes`, we can see the structure of the JSON response as well as details of possible parameters for the request. In this case, we see that the first parameter is `pretty`, which toggles whether the JSON is returned with pretty indentation for easier reading.

We can try this out by using `https://<your master ip>/api/v1/nodes/`.

By default, we'll see a JSON response with pretty indentation enabled. The response should have a list of all the nodes currently in our cluster.

Now, let's try tweaking the `pretty` request parameter you just learned about. Use `https://<your master ip>/api/v1/nodes/?pretty=false`.

Now we have the same response output, but with no indentation. This is a great resource for exploring the API and learning how to use various function calls to get more information and interact with your cluster programmatically.

# Command line

The `kubectl.sh` script has commands to explore our cluster and the workloads running on it. We will be using this command throughout the book, so let's take a second to set up our environment. We can do so by making the script executable and putting it on our PATH, in the following manner:

```
$ cd /home/<Username>/kubernetes/cluster
$ chmod +x kubectl.sh
$ export PATH=$PATH:/home/<Username>/kubernetes/cluster
$ ln -s kubectl.sh kubectl
```

You may choose to download the kubernetes folder outside your home folder, so modify the preceding commands as appropriate.

It is also a good idea to make the changes permanent by adding the export command to the end of your .bashrc file in your home directory.

Now that we have `kubectl` on our path, we can start working with it. It has quite a few commands. Since we have not spun up any applications yet, most of these commands will not be very interesting. However, we can explore with two commands right away.

First, we have already seen the `cluster-info` command during initialization, but we can run it again at any time with the following:

```
$ kubectl cluster-info
```

Another useful command is `get`. The `get` command can be used to see currently running **services**, **pods**, **replication controllers**, and a lot more. Here are the three examples that are useful right out of the gate:

- Listing the nodes in our cluster:

  ```
  $ kubectl get nodes
  ```

- List cluster events:

  ```
  $ kubectl get events
  ```

- Finally, we can see any services that are running in the cluster as follows:

```
$ kubectl get services
```

To start with, we will only see one service, named `kubernetes`. This service is the core API server, monitoring and logging services for the pods and cluster.

# Services running on the master

Let's dig a little bit deeper into our new cluster and its core services. By default, machines are named with the `kubernetes-` prefix. We can modify this using `$KUBE_GCE_INSTANCE_PREFIX` before a cluster is spun up. For the cluster we just started, the master should be named `kubernetes-master`. We can use the `gcloud` command-line utility to SSH into the machine. The following command will start an SSH session with the master node. Be sure to substitute your project ID and zone to match your environment. Also, note that you can launch SSH from the Google Cloud console using the following syntax:

```
$ gcloud compute --project "<Your project ID>" ssh --zone "<your gce
zone>" "kubernetes-master"
```

Once we are logged in, we should get a standard shell prompt. Let's run the familiar `sudo docker ps` command.

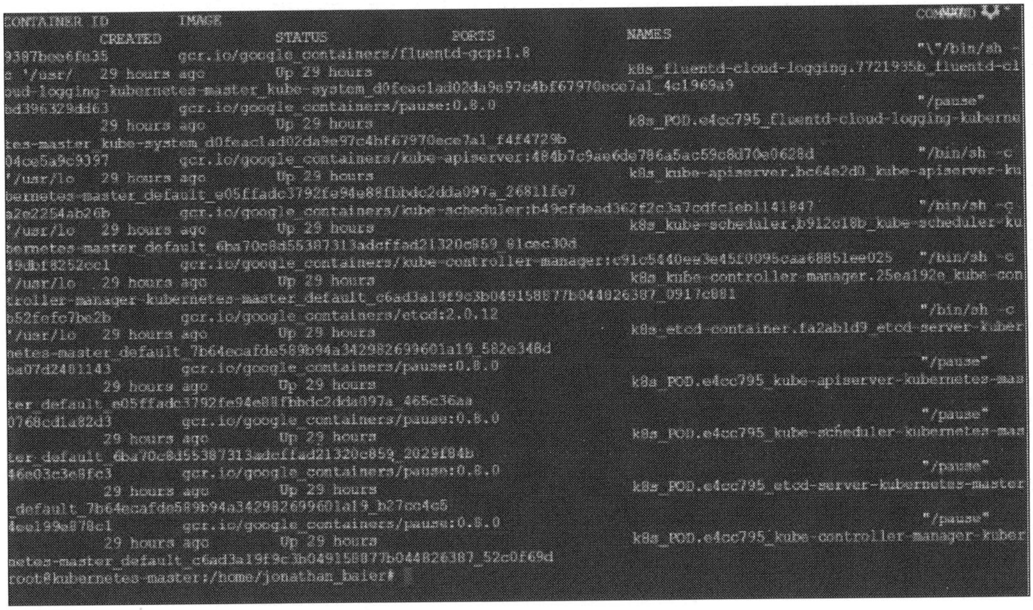

Figure 1.13. Master container listing

Even though we have not deployed any applications on Kubernetes yet, we note that there are several containers already running. The following is a brief description of each container:

- `fluentd-gcp`: This container collects and sends the cluster logs file to the Google Cloud Logging service.

- `kube-ui`: This is the UI that we saw earlier.

- `kube-controller-manager`: The controller manager controls a variety of cluster functions. Ensuring accurate and up-to-date replication is one of its vital roles. Additionally, it monitors, manages, and discovers new nodes. Finally, it manages and updates service endpoints.

- `kube-apiserver`: This container runs the API server. As we explored in the Swagger interface, this RESTful API allows us to create, query, update, and remove various components of our Kubernetes cluster.

- `kube-scheduler`: The scheduler takes unscheduled pods and binds them to nodes based on the current scheduling algorithm.

- `etcd`: This runs the **etcd** software built by CoreOS. `etcd` is a distributed and consistent key-value store. This is where the Kubernetes cluster state is stored, updated, and retrieved by various components of K8s.

- `pause`: The `Pause` container is often referred to as the pod infrastructure container and is used to set up and hold the networking namespace and resource limits for each pod.

 Figure 2.1 in the next chapter will also show how a few of these services work together.

To exit the SSH session, simply type `exit` at the prompt.

# Services running on the minions

We could SSH to one of the minions, but since Kubernetes schedules workloads across the cluster, we would not see all the containers on a single minion. However, we can look at the pods running on all the minions using the `kubectl` command:

```
$ kubectl get pods
```

Since we have not started any applications on the cluster yet, we don't see any pods. However, there are actually several system pods running pieces of the Kubernetes infrastructure. We can see these pods by specifying the `kube-system` namespace. We will explore namespaces and their significance later, but for now, the `--namespace=kube-system` command can be used to look at these K8s system resources as follows:

```
$ kubectl get pods --namespace=kube-system
```

We should see something similar to the following:

```
etcd-server
fluentd-cloud-logging
kube-apiserver
kube-controller-manager
kube-scheduler
kube-ui
kube-dns
monitoring-heapster
monitoring-influx-grafana
```

The first six should look familiar. These are additional pieces of the services we saw running on the master. The final three are services we have not seen yet. `kube-dns` provides the DNS and service discovery plumbing. `monitoring-heapster` is the system used to monitor resource usage across the cluster. `monitoring-influx-grafana` provides the database and user interface we saw earlier for monitoring the infrastructure.

If we did SSH into a random minion, we would see several containers that run across a few of these pods. A sample might look like the image here:

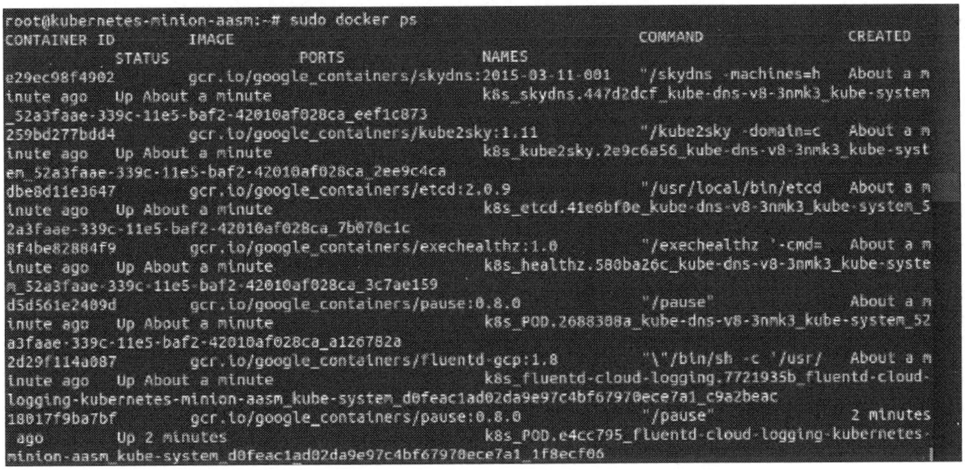

```
root@kubernetes-minion-aasm:~# sudo docker ps
CONTAINER ID        IMAGE                                              COMMAND                CREATED
            STATUS              PORTS               NAMES
e29ec98f4902        gcr.io/google_containers/skydns:2015-03-11-001   "/skydns -machines=h   About a m
inute ago   Up About a minute                       k8s_skydns.447d2dcf_kube-dns-v8-3nmk3_kube-system
_52a3faae-339c-11e5-baf2-42010af028ca_eef1c873
259bd277bdd4        gcr.io/google_containers/kube2sky:1.11           "/kube2sky -domain=c   About a m
inute ago   Up About a minute                       k8s_kube2sky.2e9c6a56_kube-dns-v8-3nmk3_kube-syst
em_52a3faae-339c-11e5-baf2-42010af028ca_2ee9c4ca
dbe8d11e3647        gcr.io/google_containers/etcd:2.0.9              "/usr/local/bin/etcd   About a m
inute ago   Up About a minute                       k8s_etcd.41e6bf0e_kube-dns-v8-3nmk3_kube-system_5
2a3faae-339c-11e5-baf2-42010af028ca_7b070c1c
8f4be82884f9        gcr.io/google_containers/exechealthz:1.0         "/exechealthz '-cmd=   About a m
inute ago   Up About a minute                       k8s_healthz.580ba26c_kube-dns-v8-3nmk3_kube-syste
m_52a3faae-339c-11e5-baf2-42010af028ca_3c7ae159
d5d561e2489d        gcr.io/google_containers/pause:0.8.0             "/pause"               About a m
inute ago   Up About a minute                       k8s_POD.2688308a_kube-dns-v8-3nmk3_kube-system_52
a3faae-339c-11e5-baf2-42010af028ca_a126782a
2d29f114a087        gcr.io/google_containers/fluentd-gcp:1.8         "\"/bin/sh -c '/usr/   About a m
inute ago   Up About a minute                       k8s_fluentd-cloud-logging.7721935b_fluentd-cloud-
logging-kubernetes-minion-aasm_kube-system_d0feac1ad02da9e97c4bf67970ece7a1_c9a2beac
18017f9ba7bf        gcr.io/google_containers/pause:0.8.0             "/pause"               2 minutes
 ago        Up 2 minutes                            k8s_POD.e4cc795_fluentd-cloud-logging-kubernetes-
minion-aasm_kube-system_d0feac1ad02da9e97c4bf67970ece7a1_1f8ecf06
```

Figure 1.14. Minion container listing

Again, we saw a similar line up of services on the master. The services we did not see on the master include the following:

- `skydns`: This uses DNS to provide a distributed service discovery utility that works with `etcd`.

- `kube2Sky`: This is the connector between `skydns` and `kubernetes`. Services in the API are monitored for changes and updated in `skydns` appropriately.

- `heapster`: This does resource usage and monitoring.

- `exechealthz`: This performs health checks on the pods.

## Tear down cluster

OK, this is our first cluster on GCE, but let's explore some other providers. To keep things simple, we need to remove the one we just created on GCE. We can tear down the cluster with one simple command:

```
$ kube-down.sh
```

# Working with other providers

By default, Kubernetes uses the GCE provider for Google Cloud. We can override this default by setting the KUBERNETES_PROVIDER environment variable. The following providers are supported with values listed in Table 1.1:

| Provider | KUBERNETES_PROVIDER value | Type |
|---|---|---|
| **Google Compute Engine** | gce | Public cloud |
| **Google Container Engine** | gke | Public cloud |
| **Amazon Web Services** | aws | Public cloud |
| **Microsoft Azure** | azure | Public cloud |
| **Hashicorp Vagrant** | vagrant | Virtual development environment |
| **VMware vSphere** | vsphere | Private cloud / on-premise virtualization |
| **Libvirt running CoreOS** | libvirt-coreos | Virtualization management tool |
| **Canonical Juju (folks behind Ubuntu)** | juju | OS service orchestration tool |

Table 1.1. Kubernetes providers

Let's try setting up the cluster on AWS. As a prerequisite, we need to have the AWS **Command Line Interface (CLI)** installed and configured for our account. AWS CLI Installation and configuration documentation can be found here:

- Installation documentation: `http://docs.aws.amazon.com/cli/latest/userguide/installing.html#install-bundle-other-os`

- Configuration documentation: `http://docs.aws.amazon.com/cli/latest/userguide/cli-chap-getting-started.html`

Then, it is a simple environment variable setting as follows:

```
$ export KUBERNETES_PROVIDER=aws
```

Again, we can use the `kube-up.sh` command to spin up the cluster as follows:

```
$ kube-up.sh
```

As with GCE, the setup activity will take a few minutes. It will stage files in **S3**, create the appropriate instances, **Virtual Private Cloud (VPC)**, security groups, and so on in our AWS account. Then, the Kubernetes cluster will be set up and started. Once everything is finished and started, we should see the cluster validation at the end of the output.

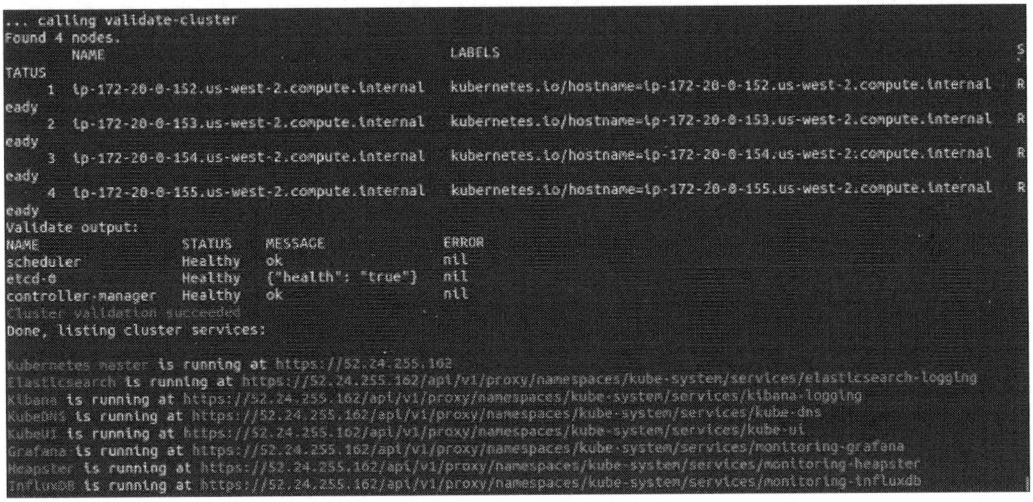

Figure 1.15. AWS cluster validation

Once again, we will SSH into master. This time, we can use the native SSH client. We'll find the key files in /home/**<username>**/.ssh:

```
$ ssh -v -i /home/<username>/.ssh/kube_aws_rsa ubuntu@<Your master IP>
```

We'll use `sudo docker ps` to explore the running containers. We should see something like the following:

```
ubuntu@ip-172-20-0-9:~$ sudo docker ps
CONTAINER ID    IMAGE                                                             CO
MMAND           CREATED         STATUS          PORTS           NAMES
32e5cab8abc8    gcr.io/google_containers/fluentd-elasticsearch:1.6               "\
"/bin/sh -c '/usr/   32 minutes ago      Up 32 minutes               k8s_fluentd-elasticsearch
.1766602_fluentd-elasticsearch-ip-172-20-0-9.us-west-2.compute.internal_kube-system_3f414d923095ffb72919d3
7e3a73ec70_7a3983a0
63c206a1c7c8    gcr.io/google_containers/kube-apiserver:1a24bc30708455afd45e7e021c037bb5               "/
bin/sh -c '/usr/lo   33 minutes ago      Up 33 minutes               k8s_kube-apiserver.2eb0e2
61_kube-apiserver-ip-172-20-0-9.us-west-2.compute.internal_default_74d07c1f7ac3445d41b0464ac4e27663_070967
09
111123bfe1f4    gcr.io/google_containers/etcd:2.0.12               "/
bin/sh -c '/usr/lo   33 minutes ago      Up 33 minutes               k8s_etcd-container.fa2ab1
d9_etcd-server-ip-172-20-0-9.us-west-2.compute.internal_default_7b64ecafde589b94a342982699601a19_d9210c69

fbcb2c07c9d1    gcr.io/google_containers/kube-controller-manager:3c2fd35b2249540e71dfd72f9453015a    "/
bin/sh -c '/usr/lo   33 minutes ago      Up 33 minutes               k8s_kube-controller-manag
er.5db11918_kube-controller-manager-ip-172-20-0-9.us-west-2.compute.internal_default_26c0ef421c27fd2b0202a
6d71859121a_4982c542
83f47fbb0a6b    gcr.io/google_containers/pause:0.8.0               "/
pause"               33 minutes ago      Up 33 minutes               k8s_POD.e4cc795_etcd-serv
er-ip-172-20-0-9.us-west-2.compute.internal_default_7b64ecafde589b94a342982699601a19_3811c07b

b69149b05846    gcr.io/google_containers/pause:0.8.0               "/
pause"               33 minutes ago      Up 33 minutes               k8s_POD.e4cc795_fluentd-e
lasticsearch-ip-172-20-0-9.us-west-2.compute.internal_kube-system_3f414d923095ffb72919d37e3a73ec70_fd353ad
7
26062fa8e60d    gcr.io/google_containers/pause:0.8.0               "/
pause"               33 minutes ago      Up 33 minutes               k8s_POD.e4cc795_kube-apis
erver-ip-172-20-0-9.us-west-2.compute.internal_default_74d07c1f7ac3445d41b0464ac4e27663_f059c853

ab5c09986160    gcr.io/google_containers/kube-scheduler:6191fb90c1fb34f751e55709a3ed8992               "/
bin/sh -c '/usr/lo   33 minutes ago      Up 33 minutes               k8s_kube-scheduler.466c08
2_kube-scheduler-ip-172-20-0-9.us-west-2.compute.internal_default_48c5c2a662e02e21ec3ff936ce6962b2_c2460bb
3
64d1e2ff124e    gcr.io/google_containers/pause:0.8.0               "/
pause"               33 minutes ago      Up 33 minutes               k8s_POD.e4cc795_kube-cont
roller-manager-ip-172-20-0-9.us-west-2.compute.internal_default_26c0ef421c27fd2b0202a6d718591 21a_9f9fc0d0

cfe3bcaa98c5    gcr.io/google_containers/pause:0.8.0               "/
pause"               33 minutes ago      Up 33 minutes               k8s_POD.e4cc795_kube-sche
```

Figure 1.16. Master container listing (AWS)

For the most part, we see the same containers as our GCE cluster had. However, instead of `fluentd-gcp` service, we see `fluentd-elasticsearch`.

On the AWS provider, **Elasticsearch** and **Kibana** are set up for us. We can find the Kibana UI by using the following syntax as URL:

```
https://<your master ip>/api/v1/proxy/namespaces/kube-system/
services/kibana-logging/#/discover
```

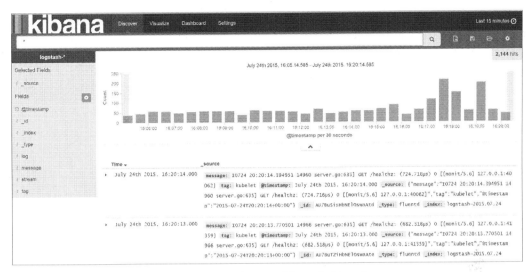

Figure 1.17. Kubernetes Kibana dashboard

# Resetting the cluster

That is a little taste of running the cluster on AWS. For the remainder of the book, I will be basing my examples on a GCE cluster. For the best experience following along, you can get back to a GCE cluster easily.

Simply tear down the AWS cluster as follows:

```
$ kube-down.sh
```

Then, create a GCE cluster again using following:

```
$ export KUBERNETES_PROVIDER=gce
$ kube-up.sh
```

# Summary

We took a very brief look at how containers work and how they lend themselves to the new architecture patterns in microservices. You should now have a better understanding of how these two forces will require a variety of operations and management tasks and how Kubernetes offers strong features to address these challenges. Finally, we created two different clusters on both GCE and AWS and explored the startup script as well as some of the built-in features of Kubernetes.

In the next chapter, we will explore the core concept and abstractions K8s provides to manage containers and full application stacks. We will also look at basic scheduling, service discovery, and health checking.

# Footnotes

[1]Malcom McLean entry on Wikipedia:
`https://en.wikipedia.org/wiki/Malcom_McLean`

[2]Martin Fowler on microservices:
`http://martinfowler.com/articles/microservices.html`

[3]Kubernetes GitHub project page: `https://github.com/kubernetes/kubernetes`

# References

- `https://en.wikipedia.org/wiki/Continuous_integration`
- `https://docs.docker.com/`
- `https://github.com/GoogleCloudPlatform/kubernetes/`

# Kubernetes – Core Concepts and Constructs

**2**

This chapter will cover the core **Kubernetes** constructs, such as **pods**, **services**, **replication controllers**, and **labels**. A few simple application examples will be included to demonstrate each construct. The chapter will also cover basic operations for your cluster. Finally, **health checks** and **scheduling** will be introduced with a few examples.

This chapter will discuss the following topics:

- Kubernetes' overall architecture
- Introduction to core Kubernetes constructs, such as pods, services, replication controllers, and labels
- Understand how labels can ease management of a Kubernetes cluster
- Understand how to monitor services and container health
- Understand how to set up scheduling constraints based on available cluster resources

## The architecture

Although **Docker** brings a helpful layer of abstraction and tooling around container management, Kubernetes brings similar assistance to orchestrating containers at scale as well as managing full application stacks.

**K8s** moves up the stack giving us constructs to deal with management at the application or service level. This gives us automation and tooling to ensure high availability, application stack, and service-wide portability. K8s also allows finer control of resource usage, such as CPU, memory, and disk space across our infrastructure.

Kubernetes provides this higher level of orchestration management by giving us key constructs to combine multiple containers, endpoints, and data into full application stacks and services. K8s then provides the tooling to manage the *when*, *where*, and *how many* of the stack and its components.

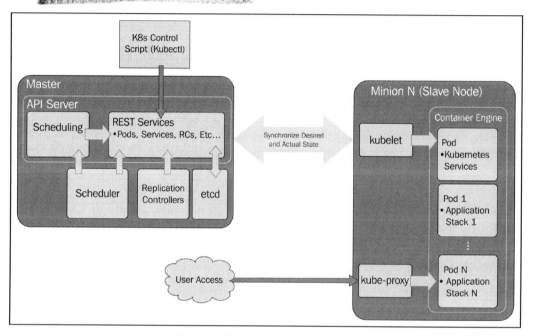

Figure 2.1. Kubernetes core architecture

In the preceding figure (Figure 2.1), we see the core architecture for Kubernetes. Most administrative interactions are done via the `kubectl` script and/or RESTful service calls to the API.

Note the ideas of the *desired state* and *actual state* carefully. This is key to how Kubernetes manages the cluster and its workloads. All the pieces of K8s are constantly working to monitor the current *actual state* and synchronize it with the *desired state* defined by the administrators via the API server or `kubectl` script. There will be times when these states do not match up, but the system is always working to reconcile the two.

# Master

Essentially, **master** is the brain of our cluster. Here, we have the core API server, which maintains RESTful web services for querying and defining our desired cluster and workload state. It's important to note that the control pane only accesses the master to initiate changes and not the nodes directly.

Additionally, the master includes the **scheduler**, which works with the API server to schedule workloads in the form of pods on the actual minion nodes. These pods include the various containers that make up our application stacks. By default, the basic Kubernetes scheduler spreads pods across the cluster and uses different nodes for matching pod replicas. Kubernetes also allows specifying necessary resources for each container, so scheduling can be altered by these additional factors.

The replication controller works with the API server to ensure that the correct number of pod replicas are running at any given time. This is exemplary of the *desired state* concept. If our replication controller is defining three replicas and our *actual state* is two copies of the pod running, then the scheduler will be invoked to add a third pod somewhere on our cluster. The same is true if there are too many pods running in the cluster at any given time. In this way, K8s is always pushing towards that *desired state*.

Finally, we have **etcd** running as a distributed configuration store. The Kubernetes state is stored here and etcd allows values to be watched for changes. Think of this as the brain's shared memory.

# Node (formerly minions)

In each node, we have a couple of components. The **kublet** interacts with the API server to update state and to start new workloads that have been invoked by the scheduler.

**Kube-proxy** provides basic load balancing and directs traffic destined for specific services to the proper pod on the backend. See the *Services* section later in this chapter.

Finally, we have some default pods, which run various infrastructure services for the node. As we explored briefly in the previous chapter, the pods include services for **Domain Name System (DNS)**, logging, and pod health checks. The default pod will run alongside our scheduled pods on every node.

Note that in v1.0, **minion** was renamed to **node**, but there are still remnants of the term minion in some of the machine naming scripts and documentation that exists on the Web. For clarity, I've added the term minion in addition to node in a few places throughout the book.

# Core constructs

Now, let's dive a little deeper and explore some of the core abstractions Kubernetes provides. These abstractions will make it easier to think about our applications and ease the burden of life cycle management, high availability, and scheduling.

# Pods

Pods allow you to keep related containers close in terms of the network and hardware infrastructure. Data can live near the application, so processing can be done without incurring a high latency from network traversal. Similarly, common data can be stored on volumes that are shared between a number of containers. Pods essentially allow you to logically group containers and pieces of our application stacks together.

While pods may run one or more containers inside, the pod itself may be one of many that is running on a Kubernetes (minion) node. As we'll see, pods give us a logical group of containers that we can then replicate, schedule, and balance service endpoints across.

## Pod example

Let's take a quick look at a pod in action. We will spin up a **Node.js** application on the cluster. You'll need a GCE cluster running for this, so see *Chapter 1, Kubernetes and Container Operations*, under the *Our first cluster* section, if you don't already have one started.

Now, let's make a directory for our definitions. In this example, I will create a folder in the /book-examples subfolder under our home directory.

```
$ mkdir book-examples
$ cd book-examples
$ mkdir 02_example
$ cd 02_example
```

Use your favorite editor to create the following file:

```
apiVersion: v1
kind: Pod
metadata:
  name: node-js-pod
spec:
  containers:
  - name: node-js-pod
    image: bitnami/apache:latest
    ports:
    - containerPort: 80
```

*Listing 2-1*: nodejs-pod.yaml

This file creates a pod name node-js-pod with the latest bitnami/apache container running on port 80. We can check this using the following command:

```
$ kubectl create -f nodejs-pod.yaml
```

The output is as follows:

```
pods/node-js-pod
```

This gives us a pod running the specified container. We can see more information on the pod by running the following command:

```
$ kubectl describe pods/node-js-pod
```

You'll see a good deal of information, such as the pod's status, IP address, and even relevant log events. You'll note the pod IP address is a private 10.x.x.x address, so we cannot access it directly from our local machine. Not to worry as the kubectl exec command mirrors Docker's exec functionality. Using this feature, we can run a command inside a pod:

```
$ kubectl exec node-js-pod -- curl <private ip address>
```

By default, this runs a command in the first container it finds, but you can select a specific one using the -c argument.

After running, the command you should see some HTML code. We'll have a prettier view later in the chapter, but for now, we can see that our pod is indeed running as expected.

# Labels

Labels give us another level of categorization, which becomes very helpful in terms of everyday operations and management. Similar to tags, labels can be used as the basis of service discovery as well as a useful grouping tool for day-to-day operations and management tasks.

Labels are just simple key-value pairs. You will see them on pods, replication controllers, services, and so on. The label acts as a selector and tells Kubernetes which resources to work with for a variety of operations. Think of it as a *filtering* option.

We will take a look at labels more in depth later in this chapter, but first, we will explore the remaining two constructs, services, and replication controllers.

# The container's afterlife

As anyone in operations can attest, failures happen all the time. Containers and pods can and will crash, become corrupted, or maybe even just get accidentally shut off by a clumsy admin poking around on one of the nodes. Strong policy and security practices like enforcing least privilege curtail some of these incidents, but "involuntary workload slaughter happens" and is simply a fact of operations.

Luckily, Kubernetes provides two very valuable constructs to keep this somber affair all tidied up behind the curtains. Services and replication controllers give us the ability to keep our applications running with little interruption and graceful recovery.

# Services

Services allow us to abstract access away from the consumers of our applications. Using a reliable endpoint, users and other programs can access pods running on your cluster seamlessly.

K8s achieves this by making sure that every node in the cluster runs a proxy named kube-proxy. As the name suggests, kube-proxy's job is to proxy communication from a service endpoint back to the corresponding pod that is running the actual application.

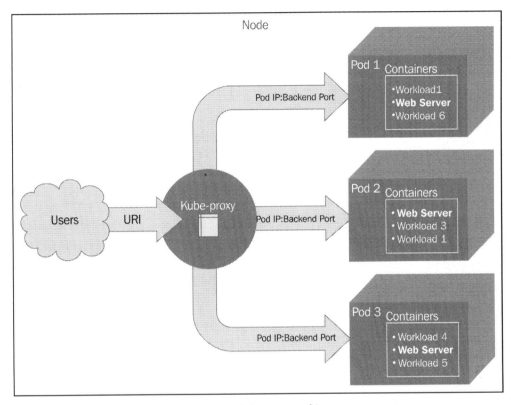

Figure 2.2. The kube-proxy architecture

Membership in the service load balancing pool is determined by the use of selectors and labels. Pods with matching labels are added to the list of candidates where the service forwards traffic. A virtual IP address and port are used as the entry point for the service, and traffic is then forwarded to a random pod on a target port defined by either K8s or your definition file.

Updates to service definitions are monitored and coordinated from the K8s cluster master and propagated to the **kube-proxy daemons** running on each node.

At the moment, kube-proxy is running on the node host itself. There are plans to containerize this and the kubelet by default in the future.

# Replication controllers

**Replication controllers (RCs)**, as the name suggests, manage the number of nodes that a pod and included container images run on. They ensure that an instance of an image is being run with the specific number of copies.

As you start to operationalize your containers and pods, you'll need a way to roll out updates, scale the number of copies running (both up and down), or simply ensure that at least one instance of your stack is always running. RCs create a high-level mechanism to make sure that things are operating correctly across the entire application and cluster.

RCs are simply charged with ensuring that you have the desired scale for your application. You define the number of pod replicas you want running and give it a template for how to create new pods. Just like services, we will use selectors and labels to define a pod's membership in a replication controller.

 Kubernetes doesn't require the strict behavior of the replication controller. In fact, version 1.1 has a **job controller** in beta that can be used for short lived workloads which allow jobs to be run to a completion state.

# Our first Kubernetes application

Before we move on, let's take a look at these three concepts in action. Kubernetes ships with a number of examples installed, but we will create a new example from scratch to illustrate some of the concepts.

We've already created a pod definition file, but as we learned, there are many advantages to running our pods via replication controllers. Again, using the `book-examples/02_example` folder we made earlier, we will create some definition files and start a cluster of Node.js servers using a replication controller approach. Additionally, we'll add a public face to it with a load-balanced service.

Use your favorite editor to create the following file:

```
apiVersion: v1
kind: ReplicationController
metadata:
  name: node-js
  labels:
    name: node-js
deployment: demo
spec:
  replicas: 3
  selector:
    name: node-js
    deployment: demo
  template:
    metadata:
      labels:
        name: node-js
    spec:
      containers:
      - name: node-js
        image: jonbaier/node-express-info:latest
        ports:
        - containerPort: 80
```

*Listing 2-2:* `nodejs-controller.yaml`

This is the first resource definition file for our cluster, so let's take a closer look. You'll note that it has four first-level elements (`kind`, `apiVersion`, `metadata`, and `spec`). These are common among all top-level Kubernetes resource definitions:

- `Kind` tells K8s what type of resource we are creating. In this case, the type is `ReplicationController`. The `kubectl` script uses a single `create` command for all types of resources. The benefit here is that you can easily create a number of resources of various types without needing to specify individual parameters for each type. However, it requires that the definition files can identify what it is they are specifying.

- `ApiVersion` simply tells Kubernetes which version of the schema we are using. All examples in this book will be on `v1`.

- `Metadata` is where we will give the resource a name and also specify labels that will be used to search and select resources for a given operation. The metadata element also allows you to create annotations, which are for nonidentifying information that might be useful for client tools and libraries.

- Finally, we have `spec`, which will vary based on the `kind` or type of resource we are creating. In this case, it's `ReplicationController`, which ensures the desired number of pods are running. The `replicas` element defines the desired number of pods, the `selector` tells the controller which pods to watch, and finally, the `template` element defines a template to launch a new pod. The `template` section contains the same pieces we saw in our pod definition earlier. An important thing to note is that the `selector` values need to match the `labels` values specified in the pod template. Remember that this matching is used to select the pods being managed.

Now, let's take a look at the service definition:

```
apiVersion: v1
kind: Service
metadata:
  name: node-js
  labels:
    name: node-js
spec:
  type: LoadBalancer
  ports:
  - port: 80
  selector:
    name: node-js
```

*Listing 2-3*: `nodejs-rc-service.yaml`

The YAML here is similar to the `ReplicationController`. The main difference is seen in the service `spec` element. Here, we define the `Service` type, listening `port`, and `selector`, which tells the `Service` proxy which pods can answer the service.

 Kubernetes supports both YAML and JSON formats for definition files.

Create the Node.js express replication controller:

```
$ kubectl create -f nodejs-controller.yaml
```

The output is as follows:

```
replicationcontrollers/node-js
```

This gives us a replication controller that ensures that three copies of the container are always running:

```
$ kubectl create -f nodejs-rc-service.yaml
```

The output is as follows:

```
services/node-js
```

On GCE, this will create an external load balancer and forwarding rules, but you may need to add additional firewall rules. In my case, the firewall was already open for port 80. However, you may need to open this port, especially if you deploy a service with ports other than 80 and 443.

OK, now we have a running service, which means that we can access the Node.js servers from a reliable URL. Let's take a look at our running services:

```
$ kubectl get services
```

The following screenshot is the result of the preceding command:

```
NAME            LABELS                                          SELECTOR
   IP(S)               PORT(S)
kubernetes      component=apiserver,provider=kubernetes         <none>
   10.0.0.1             443/TCP
node-js         name=node-js                                    name=node-js
   10.0.48.73          80/TCP

   130.211.186.84
```

Figure 2.3. Services listing

In the preceding figure (Figure 2.3), you should note that the **node-js** service running and, in the **IP(S)** column, you should have both a private and a public (**130.211.186.84** in the screenshot) IP address. Let's see if we can connect by opening up the public address in a browser:

```
Host: node-js-u26fd
Running OS: linux
Uptime: 525274
Network Information: 10.244.1.17, fe80::42:aff:fef4:111
DNS Servers: 10.0.0.10,169.254.169.254,10.240.0.1
```

Figure 2.4. Container info application

You should see something like Figure 2.4. If we visit multiple times, you should note that the container name changes. Essentially, the service load balancer is rotating between available pods on the backend.

Browsers usually cache web pages, so to really see the container name change you may need to clear your cache or use a proxy like this one: `https://hide.me/en/proxy`

Let's try playing chaos monkey a bit and kill off a few containers to see what Kubernetes does. In order to do this, we need to see where the pods are actually running. First, let's list our pods:

```
$ kubectl get pods
```

The following screenshot is the result of the preceding command:

| NAME | READY | STATUS | RESTARTS | AGE |
|------|-------|--------|----------|-----|
| node-js-1fxoy | 1/1 | Running | 0 | 1d |
| node-js-m4w4a | 1/1 | Running | 0 | 1d |
| node-js-sjc03 | 1/1 | Running | 0 | 1d |

Figure 2.5. Currently running pods

Now, let's get some more details on one of the pods running a `node-js` container. You can do this with the `describe` command with one of the pod names listed in the last command:

```
$ kubectl describe pod/node-js-sjc03
```

The following screenshot is the result of the preceding command:

```
Name:                          node-js-sjc03
Namespace:                     default
Image(s):                      petegoo/node-express-sample:latest
Node:                          kubernetes-minion-aqdf/10.240.142.178
Labels:                        name=node-js
Status:                        Running
Reason:
Message:
IP:                            10.244.0.10
Replication Controllers:       node-js (3/3 replicas created)
Containers:
  node-js:
    Image:       petegoo/node-express-sample:latest
    Limits:
      cpu:                     100m
    State:                     Running
      Started:                 Tue, 28 Jul 2015 16:57:33 -0400
    Ready:                     True
    Restart Count:             0
Conditions:
  Type           Status
  Ready          True
No events.
```

Figure 2.6. Pod description

You should see the preceding output. The information we need is the **Node:** section. Let's use the node name to **SSH** (short for **Secure Shell**) into the (minion) node running this workload:

```
$ gcloud compute --project "<Your project ID>" ssh --zone "<your gce
zone>" "<Node from pod describe>"
```

Once SSHed into the node, if we run a `sudo docker ps` command, we should see at least two containers: one running the `pause` image and one running the actual `node-express-info` image. You may see more if the K8s scheduled more than one replica on this node. Let's grab the container ID of the `jonbaier/node-express-info` image (not `gcr.io/google_containers/pause`) and kill it off to see what happens. Save this container ID somewhere for later:

```
$ sudo docker ps --filter="name=node-js"

$ sudo docker stop <node-express container id>

$ sudo docker rm <container id>

$ sudo docker ps --filter="name=node-js"
```

Unless you are really quick you'll probably note that there is still a `node-express-info` container running, but look closely and you'll note that the `container id` is different and the creation time stamp shows only a few seconds ago. If you go back to the service URL, it is functioning like normal. Go ahead and exit the SSH session for now.

Here, we are already seeing Kubernetes playing the role of on-call operations ensuring that our application is always running.

Let's see if we can find any evidence of the outage. Go to the **Events** page in the Kubernetes UI. You can find it on the main K8s dashboard under **Events** in the **Views** menu. Alternatively, you can just use the following URL, adding your `master ip`:

```
https://<your master ip>/api/v1/proxy/namespaces/kube-system/
services/kube-ui/#/dashboard/events
```

You will see a screen similar to the following screenshot:

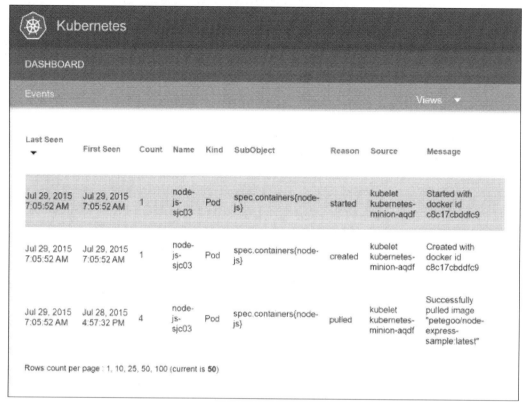

Figure 2.7. Kubernetes UI event page

You should see three recent events. First, Kubernetes pulls the image. Second, it creates a new container with the pulled image. Finally, it starts that container again. You'll note that, from the time stamps, this all happens in less than a second. Time taken may vary based on cluster size and image pulls, but the recovery is very quick.

# More on labels

As mentioned previously, labels are just simple key-value pairs. They are available on pods, replication controllers, services, and more. If you recall our service YAML, in *Listing 2-3*: `nodejs-rc-service.yaml`, there was a `selector` attribute. The `selector` tells Kubernetes which labels to use in finding pods to forward traffic for that service.

K8s allows users to work with labels directly on replication controllers and services. Let's modify our replicas and services to include a few more labels. Once again, use your favorite editor and create these two files as follows:

```
apiVersion: v1
kind: ReplicationController
metadata:
  name: node-js-labels
  labels:
    name: node-js-labels
    app: node-js-express
    deployment: test
spec:
  replicas: 3
  selector:
    name: node-js-labels
    app: node-js-express
    deployment: test
  template:
    metadata:
      labels:
        name: node-js-labels
        app: node-js-express
        deployment: test
    spec:
      containers:
      - name: node-js-labels
        image: jonbaier/node-express-info:latest
        ports:
        - containerPort: 80
```

*Listing 2-4*: `nodejs-labels-controller.yaml`

```
apiVersion: v1
kind: Service
metadata:
  name: node-js-labels
  labels:
    name: node-js-labels
    app: node-js-express
    deployment: test
spec:
  type: LoadBalancer
  ports:
  - port: 80
```

```
selector:
    name: node-js-labels
    app: node-js-express
    deployment: test
```

*Listing 2-5:* `nodejs-labels-service.yaml`

Create the replication controller and service as follows:

```
$ kubectl create -f nodejs-labels-controller.yaml
$ kubectl create -f nodejs-labels-service.yaml
```

Let's take a look at how we can use labels in everyday management. The following table shows us the options to select labels:

| Operators | Description | Example |
|-----------|-------------|---------|
| `= or ==` | You can use either style to select keys with values equal to the string on the right | `name = apache` |
| `!=` | Select keys with values that do not equal the string on the right | `Environment != test` |
| `In` | Select resources whose labels have keys with values in this set | `tier in (web, app)` |
| `Notin` | Select resources whose labels have keys with values not in this set | `tier not in (lb, app)` |
| `<Key name>` | Use a key name only to select resources whose labels contain this key | `tier` |

Table 1: Label selectors

Let's try looking for replicas with `test` deployments:

```
$ kubectl get rc-l deployment=test
```

The following screenshot is the result of the preceding command:

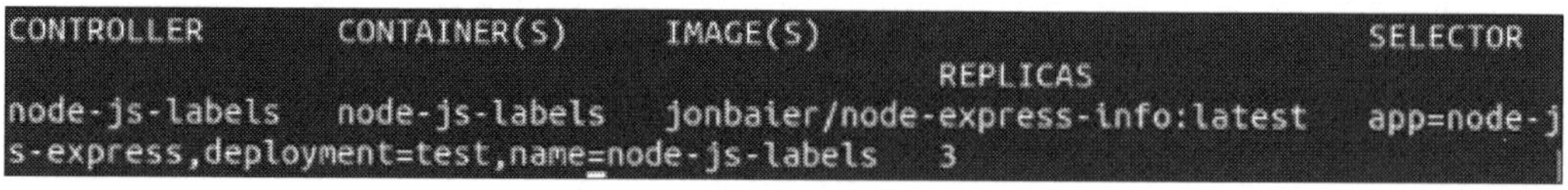

Figure 2.8. Replication controller listing

You'll notice that it only returns the replication controller we just started. How about services with a label named component? Use the following command:

```
$ kubectl get services -l component
```

The following screenshot is the result of the preceding command:

```
NAME            LABELS                                      SELECTOR   IP(S)      POR
T(S)
kubernetes      component=apiserver,provider=kubernetes     <none>     10.0.0.1   443
/TCP
```

Figure 2.9. Listing of services with a label named "component"

Here, we see the core Kubernetes service only. Finally, let's just get the node-js servers we started in this chapter. See the following command:

```
$ kubectl get services -l "name in (node-js,node-js-labels)"
```

The following screenshot is the result of the preceding command:

```
NAME            LABELS                                                            SELECTOR
                                IP(S)           PORT(S)
node-js         name=node-js                                                      name=node-js
                                10.0.103.215    80/TCP

                                104.154.67.99
node-js-labels  app=node-js-express,deployment=test,name=node-js-labels          app=node-js-express,dep
loyment=test,name=node-js-labels  10.0.176.43   80/TCP

                                146.148.56.25
```

Figure 2.10. Listing of services with a label name and a value of "node-js" or "nodejs-labels"

Additionally, we can perform management tasks across a number of pods and services. For example, we can kill all replication controllers that are part of the demo deployment (if we had any running) as follows:

```
$ kubectl delete rc -l deployment=demo
```

Otherwise, kill all services that are not part of a production or test deployment (again, if we had any running), as follows:

```
$ kubectl delete service -l "deployment notin (test, production)"
```

It's important to note that while label selection is quite helpful in day-to-day management tasks it does require proper deployment hygiene on our part. We need to make sure that we have a tagging standard and that it is actively followed in the resource definition files for everything we run on Kubernetes.

While we used service definition YAML files to create our services thus far, you can actually create them using a `kubectl` command only. To try this out, first run the `get pods` command and get one of the `node-js` pod names. Next, use the following `expose` command to create a service endpoint for just that pod:

```
$ kubectl expose pods/node-js-gxkix --port=80
--name=testing-vip --create-external-load-balancer=true
```

This will create a service named `testing-vip` and also a public `vip` (load balancer IP) that can be used to access this pod over port 80. There's a number of other optional parameters that can be used. These can be found with the following:

```
kubectl expose --help
```

# Health checks

Kubernetes provides two layers of health checking. First, in the form of HTTP or TCP checks, K8s can attempt to connect to a particular endpoint and give a status of healthy on a successful connection. Second, application-specific health checks can be performed using command line scripts.

Let's take a look at a few health checks in action. First, we'll create a new controller with a health check:

```
apiVersion: v1
kind: ReplicationController
metadata:
  name: node-js
  labels:
    name: node-js
spec:
  replicas: 3
  selector:
    name: node-js
  template:
    metadata:
      labels:
        name: node-js
    spec:
      containers:
      - name: node-js
        image: jonbaier/node-express-info:latest
        ports:
```

```
      - containerPort: 80
    livenessProbe:
      # An HTTP health check
      httpGet:
        path: /status/
        port: 80
      initialDelaySeconds: 30
      timeoutSeconds: 1
```

*Listing 2-6:* `nodejs-health-controller.yaml`

Note the addition of the `livenessprobe` element. This is our core health check element. From there, we can specify `httpGet`, `tcpScoket`, or `exec`. In this example, we use `httpGet` to perform a simple check for a URI on our container. The probe will check the path and port specified and restart the pod if it doesn't successfully return.

Status codes between `200` and `399` are all considered healthy by the probe.

Finally, `initialDelaySeconds` gives us the flexibility to delay health checks until the pod has finished initializing. `timeoutSeconds` is simply the timeout value for the probe.

Let's use our new health check-enabled controller to replace the old `node-js` RC. We can do this using the `replace` command, which will replace the replication controller definition:

**$ kubectl replace -f nodejs-health-controller.yaml**

Replacing the RC on it's own won't replace our containers because it still has three healthy pods from our first run. Let's kill off those pods and let the updated `ReplicationController` replace them with containers that have health checks.

**$ kubectl delete pods -l name=node-js**

Now, after waiting a minute or two, we can list the pods in an RC and grab one of the pod IDs to inspect a bit deeper with the `describe` command:

**$ kubectl describe rc/node-js**

The following screenshot is the result of the preceding command:

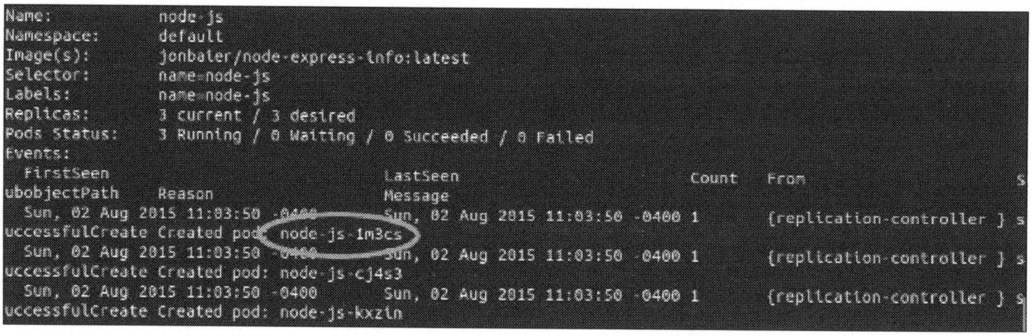

```
Name:           node-js
Namespace:      default
Image(s):       jonbaier/node-express-info:latest
Selector:       name=node-js
Labels:         name=node-js
Replicas:       3 current / 3 desired
Pods Status:    3 Running / 0 Waiting / 0 Succeeded / 0 Failed
Events:
  FirstSeen                     LastSeen                        Count   From                            S
ubobjectPath    Reason                  Message
  Sun, 02 Aug 2015 11:03:50 -0400       Sun, 02 Aug 2015 11:03:50 -0400 1       {replication-controller } s
uccessfulCreate Created pod: node-js-1m3cs
  Sun, 02 Aug 2015 11:03:50 -0400       Sun, 02 Aug 2015 11:03:50 -0400 1       {replication-controller } s
uccessfulCreate Created pod: node-js-cj4s3
  Sun, 02 Aug 2015 11:03:50 -0400       Sun, 02 Aug 2015 11:03:50 -0400 1       {replication-controller } s
uccessfulCreate Created pod: node-js-kxzln
```

Figure 2.11. Description of "node-js" replication controller

Then, using the following command for one of the pods:

```
$ kubectl describe pods/node-js-1m3cs
```

The following screenshot is the result of the preceding command:

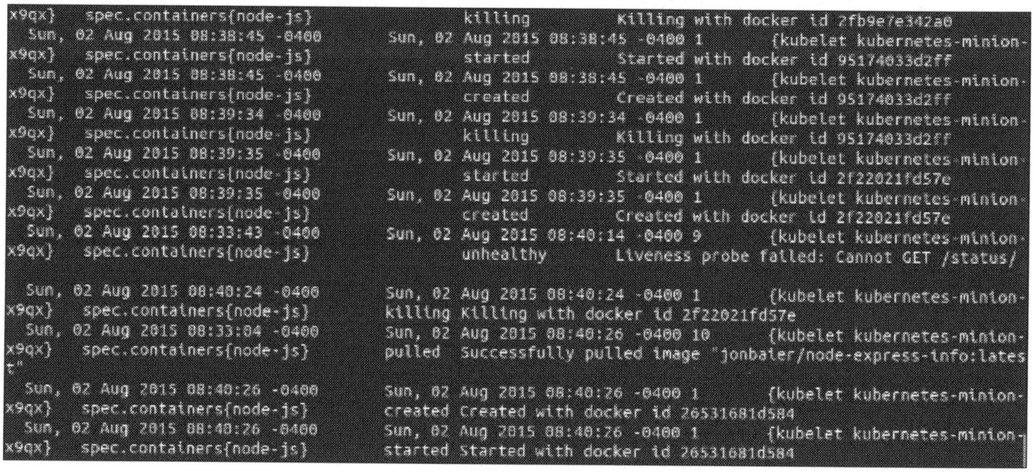

```
x9qx}   spec.containers{node-js}                        killing         Killing with docker id 2fb9e7e342a0
  Sun, 02 Aug 2015 08:38:45 -0400       Sun, 02 Aug 2015 08:38:45 -0400 1       {kubelet kubernetes-minion-
x9qx}   spec.containers{node-js}                        started         Started with docker id 95174033d2ff
  Sun, 02 Aug 2015 08:38:45 -0400       Sun, 02 Aug 2015 08:38:45 -0400 1       {kubelet kubernetes-minion-
x9qx}   spec.containers{node-js}                        created         Created with docker id 95174033d2ff
  Sun, 02 Aug 2015 08:39:34 -0400       Sun, 02 Aug 2015 08:39:34 -0400 1       {kubelet kubernetes-minion-
x9qx}   spec.containers{node-js}                        killing         Killing with docker id 95174033d2ff
  Sun, 02 Aug 2015 08:39:35 -0400       Sun, 02 Aug 2015 08:39:35 -0400 1       {kubelet kubernetes-minion-
x9qx}   spec.containers{node-js}                        started         Started with docker id 2f22021fd57e
  Sun, 02 Aug 2015 08:39:35 -0400       Sun, 02 Aug 2015 08:39:35 -0400 1       {kubelet kubernetes-minion-
x9qx}   spec.containers{node-js}                        created         Created with docker id 2f22021fd57e
  Sun, 02 Aug 2015 08:33:43 -0400       Sun, 02 Aug 2015 08:40:14 -0400 9       {kubelet kubernetes-minion-
x9qx}   spec.containers{node-js}                        unhealthy       Liveness probe failed: Cannot GET /status/

  Sun, 02 Aug 2015 08:40:24 -0400       Sun, 02 Aug 2015 08:40:24 -0400 1       {kubelet kubernetes-minion-
x9qx}   spec.containers{node-js}        killing Killing with docker id 2f22021fd57e
  Sun, 02 Aug 2015 08:33:04 -0400       Sun, 02 Aug 2015 08:40:26 -0400 10      {kubelet kubernetes-minion-
x9qx}   spec.containers{node-js}        pulled  Successfully pulled image "jonbaier/node-express-info:lates
t"
  Sun, 02 Aug 2015 08:40:26 -0400       Sun, 02 Aug 2015 08:40:26 -0400 1       {kubelet kubernetes-minion-
x9qx}   spec.containers{node-js}        created Created with docker id 26531681d584
  Sun, 02 Aug 2015 08:40:26 -0400       Sun, 02 Aug 2015 08:40:26 -0400 1       {kubelet kubernetes-minion-
x9qx}   spec.containers{node-js}        started Started with docker id 26531681d584
```

Figure 2.12. Description of "node-js-1m3cs" pod

Depending on your timing, you will likely have a number of events for the pod. Within a minute or two, you'll note a pattern of *killing*, *started*, and *created* events repeating over and over again. You should also see an unhealthy event described as **Liveness probe failed: Cannot GET /status/**. This is our health check failing because we don't have a page responding at `/status`.

You may note that if you open a browser to the service load balancer address, it still responds with a page. You can find the load balancer IP with a `kubectl get services` command.

This is happening for a number of reasons. First, the health check is simply failing because /status doesn't exist, but the page where the service is pointed is still functioning normally. Second, the livenessProbe is only charged with restarting the container on a health check fail. There is a separate readinessProbe that will remove a container from the pool of pods answering service endpoints.

Let's modify the health check for a page that does exist in our container, so we have a proper health check. We'll also add a readiness check and point it to the nonexistent status page. Open the nodejs-health-controller.yaml file and modify the spec section to match *Listing 2-7* and save it as nodejs-health-controller-2.yaml.

```yaml
apiVersion: v1
kind: ReplicationController
metadata:
  name: node-js
  labels:
    name: node-js
spec:
  replicas: 3
  selector:
    name: node-js
  template:
    metadata:
      labels:
        name: node-js
    spec:
      containers:
      - name: node-js
        image: jonbaier/node-express-info:latest
        ports:
        - containerPort: 80
        livenessProbe:
          # An HTTP health check
          httpGet:
            path: /status/
            port: 80
          initialDelaySeconds: 30
          timeoutSeconds: 1
        readinessProbe:
          # An HTTP health check
          httpGet:
            path: /status/
            port: 80
          initialDelaySeconds: 30
          timeoutSeconds: 1
```

*Listing 2-7*: `nodejs-health-controller-2.yaml`

This time, we will delete the old RC, which will kill the pods with it, and create a new RC with our updated YAML file.

```
$ kubectl delete rc -l name=node-js
$ kubectl create -f nodejs-health-controller-2.yaml
```

Now when we describe one of the pods, we only see the creation of the pod and the container. However, you'll note that the service load balancer IP no longer works. If we run the `describe` command on one of the new nodes we'll note a **Readiness probe failed** error message, but the pod itself continues running. If we change the readiness probe path to `path: /`, we will again be able to fulfill requests from the main service. Open up `nodejs-health-controller-2.yaml` in an editor and make that update now. Then, once again remove and recreate the replication controller:

```
$ kubectl delete rc -l name=node-js
$ kubectl create -f nodejs-health-controller-2.yaml
```

Now the load balancer IP should work once again. Keep these pods around as we will use them again in *Chapter 3, Core Concepts – Networking, Storage, and Advanced Services*.

# TCP checks

Kubernetes also supports health checks via simple TCP socket checks and also with custom command-line scripts. The following snippets are examples of what both use cases look like in the YAML file:

```
livenessProbe:
  exec:
    command:
    -/usr/bin/health/checkHttpServce.sh
  initialDelaySeconds:90
  timeoutSeconds: 1
```

*Listing 2-8: Health check using command-line script*

```
livenessProbe:
  tcpSocket:
    port: 80
  initialDelaySeconds: 15
  timeoutSeconds: 1
```

*Listing 2-9: Health check using simple TCP Socket connection*

# Life cycle hooks or graceful shutdown

As you run into failures in real-life scenarios, you may find that you want to take additional action before containers are shutdown or right after they are started. Kubernetes actually provides life cycle hooks for just this kind of use case.

The following example controller definition defines both a `postStart` and a `preStop` action to take place before Kubernetes moves the container into the next stage of its life cycle[1]:

```
apiVersion: v1
kind: ReplicationController
metadata:
  name: apache-hook
  labels:
    name: apache-hook
spec:
  replicas: 3
  selector:
    name: apache-hook
  template:
    metadata:
      labels:
        name: apache-hook
    spec:
      containers:
      - name: apache-hook
        image: bitnami/apache:latest
        ports:
        - containerPort: 80
        lifecycle:
          postStart:
            httpGet:
              path: http://my.registration-server.com/register/
              port: 80
          preStop:
            exec:
              command: ["/usr/local/bin/apachectl","-k","graceful-
                stop"]
```

*Listing 2-10*: `apache-hooks-controller.yaml`

You'll note for the postStart hook we define an httpGet action, but for the preStop hook, I define an exec action. Just as with our health checks, the httpGet action attempts to make an HTTP call to the specific endpoint and port combination while the exec action runs a local command in the container.

The httpGet and exec action are both supported for the postStart and preStop hooks. In the case of preStop, a parameter named reason will be sent to the handler as a parameter. See the following table (Table 2.1) for valid values:

| Reason parameter | Failure Description |
| --- | --- |
| **Delete** | Delete command issued via kubectl or the API |
| **Health** | Health check fails |
| **Dependency** | Dependency failure such as a disk mount failure or a default infrastructure pod crash |

Table 2.1. Valid preStop reasons[1]

It's important to note that hook calls are delivered *at least once*. Therefore, any logic in the action should gracefully handles multiple calls. Another important note is that postStart runs before a pod enters its ready state. If the hook itself fails, the pod will be considered unhealthy.

# Application scheduling

Now that we understand how to run containers in pods and even recover from failure, it may be useful to understand how new containers are scheduled on our cluster nodes.

As mentioned earlier, the default behavior for the Kubernetes scheduler is to spread container replicas across the nodes in our cluster. In the absence of all other constraints, the scheduler will place new pods on nodes with the least number of other pods belonging to matching services or replication controllers.

Additionally, the scheduler provides the ability to add constraints based on resources available to the node. Today, that includes minimum CPU and memory allocations. In terms of Docker, these use the **cpu-shares** and **memory limit flags** under the covers.

When additional constraints are defined, Kubernetes will check a node for available resources. If a node does not meet all the constraints, it will move to the next. If no nodes can be found that meet the criteria, then we will see a scheduling error in the logs.

The Kubernetes roadmap also has plans to support networking and storage. Because scheduling is such an important piece of overall operations and management for containers, we should expect to see many additions in this area as the project grows.

# Scheduling example

Let's take a look at a quick example of setting some resource limits. If we look at our K8s dashboard, we can get a quick snapshot of the current state of resource usage on our cluster using `https://<your master ip>`/api/v1/proxy/namespaces/kube-system/services/kube-ui, as shown in the following screenshot:

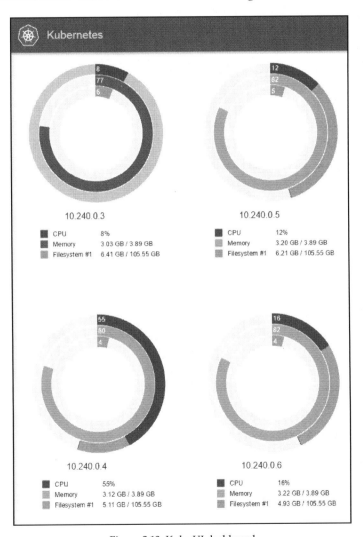

Figure 2.13. Kube UI dashboard

In this case, we have fairly low CPU utilization, but a decent chunk of memory in use. Let's see what happens when I try to spin up a few more pods, but this time, we will request 512 Mi for memory and 1500 m for the CPU. We'll use 1500 m to specify 1.5 CPUs, since each node only has 1 CPU, this should result in failure. Here's an example of RC definition:

```
apiVersion: v1
kind: ReplicationController
metadata:
  name: node-js-constraints
  labels:
    name: node-js-constraints
spec:
  replicas: 3
  selector:
    name: node-js-constraints
  template:
    metadata:
      labels:
        name: node-js-constraints
    spec:
      containers:
      - name: node-js-constraints
        image: jonbaier/node-express-info:latest
        ports:
        - containerPort: 80
        resources:
        limits:
          memory: "512Mi"
          cpu: "1500m"
```

*Listing 2-11*: `nodejs-constraints-controller.yaml`

To open the preceding file, use the following command:

```
$ kubectl create -f nodejs-constraints-controller.yaml
```

The replication controller completes successfully, but if we run a `get pods` command, we'll note the `node-js-constraints` pods are stuck in a pending state. If we look a little closer with the `describe pods/<pod-id>` command, we'll note a scheduling error:

```
$ kubectl get pods
$ kubectl describe pods/<pod-id>
```

The following screenshot is the result of the preceding command:

```
Namespace:                          default
Image(s):                           bitnami/apache:latest
Node:                               /
Labels:                             name=node-js-constraints
Status:                             Pending
Reason:
Message:
IP:
Replication Controllers:            node-js-constraints (3/3 replicas created)
Containers:
  node-js-constraints:
    Image:        bitnami/apache:latest
    Limits:
      cpu:           1500m
      memory:        512Mi
    State:          Waiting
    Ready:          False
    Restart Count:  0
Events:
  FirstSeen                         LastSeen                       Count   From             Subobject
Path    Reason                      Message
  Fri, 07 Aug 2015 16:18:18 -0400   Fri, 07 Aug 2015 16:17:22 -0400 28     {scheduler }               f
ailedScheduling Failed for reason PodFitsResources and possibly others
```

Figure 2.14. Pod description

Note that the **failedScheduling** error listed in events is accompanied by **Failed for reason PodFitsResources and possibly others** on our screen. As you can see, Kubernetes could not find a fit in the cluster that met all the constraints we defined.

If we now modify our CPU constraint down to 500 m, and then recreate our replication controller, we should have all three pods running within a few moments.

# Summary

We've taken a look at the overall architecture for Kubernetes as well as the core constructs provided to build your services and application stacks. You should have a better understanding of how these abstractions make it easier to manage the life cycle of your stack and/or services as a whole and not just the individual components. Additionally, we took a first-hand look at how to manage some simple day-to-day tasks using pods, services, and replication controllers. We also looked at how to use Kubernetes to automatically respond to outages via health checks. Finally, we explored the Kubernetes scheduler and some of the constraints users can specify to influence scheduling placement.

# Footnotes

[1]`https://github.com/GoogleCloudPlatform/kubernetes/blob/release-1.0/docs/user-guide/container-environment.md#container-hooks`

# 3
# Core Concepts – Networking, Storage, and Advanced Services

In this chapter, we will be covering how the Kubernetes cluster handles networking and how it differs from other approaches. We will be describing the three requirements for Kubernetes networking solutions and exploring why these are key to ease of operations. Further, we will take a deeper dive into services and how the Kubernetes proxy works on each node. Towards the end, we will take a look at storage concerns and how we can persist data across pods and the container life cycle. Finishing up, we will see a brief overview of some higher level isolation features for multitenancy.

This chapter will discuss the following:

- Kubernetes networking
- Advanced services concepts
- Service discovery
- DNS
- Persistent storage
- Namespace limits and quotas

# Kubernetes networking

Networking is a vital concern for production-level operations. At a service level, we need a reliable way for our application components to find and communicate with each other. Introduce containers and clustering into the mix and things get more complex as we now have multiple networking namespaces to bear in mind. Communication and discovery now becomes a feat that must traverse container IP space, host networking, and sometimes even multiple data center network topologies.

Kubernetes benefits here from getting its ancestry from the clustering tools used by Google for the past decade. Networking is one area where Google has outpaced the competition with one of the largest networks on the planet. Early on, Google built its own hardware switches and **Software-defined Networking (SDN)** to give them more control, redundancy, and efficiency in their day-to-day network operations[1]. Many of the lessons learned from running and networking two billion containers per week have been distilled into Kubernetes and informed how K8s networking is done.

Networking in Kubernetes requires that each pod have its own IP address. Implementation details may vary based on the underlying infrastructure provider. However, all implementations must adhere to some basic rules. First and second, Kubernetes does not allow the use of **Network Address Translation (NAT)** for container-to-container or for container-to-node (minion) traffic. Further, the internal container IP address must match the IP address that is used to communicate with it.

These rules keep much of the complexity out of our networking stack and ease the design of the applications. Further, it eliminates the need to redesign network communication in legacy applications that are migrated from existing infrastructure. Finally, in greenfield applications, it allows for greater scale in handling hundreds, or even thousands, of services and application communication.

K8s achieves this pod-wide IP magic by using a **placeholder**. Remember that pause container we saw in *Chapter 1, Kubernetes and Container Operations*, under the *Services running on the master* section. That is often referred to as a **pod infrastructure container**, and it has the important job of reserving the network resources for our application containers that will be started later on. Essentially, the pause container holds the networking namespace and IP address for the entire pod and can be used by all the containers running within.

# Networking comparisons

In getting a better understanding of networking in containers, it can be instructive to look at other approaches to container networking.

# Docker

The **Docker Engine** by default uses a *bridged* networking mode. In this mode, the container has its own networking namespace and is then bridged via virtual interfaces to the host (or node in the case of K8s) network.

In the *bridged* mode, two containers can use the same IP range because they are completely isolated. Therefore, service communication requires some additional port mapping through the host side of network interfaces.

Docker also supports a *host* mode, which allows the containers to use the host network stack. Performance is greatly benefited since it removes a level of network virtualization; however, you lose the security of having an isolated network namespace.

Finally, Docker supports a *container* mode, which shares a network namespace between two containers. The containers will share the namespace and IP address, so containers cannot use the same ports.

In all these scenarios, we are still on a single machine, and outside of a host mode, the container IP space is not available outside that machine. Connecting containers across two machines then requires **Network Address Translation (NAT)** and **port mapping** for communication.

# Docker plugins (libnetwork)

In order to address the cross-machine communication issue, Docker has released new network plugins, which just moved out of experimental support as we went to press. This plugin allows networks to be created independent of the containers themselves. In this way, containers can join the same existing *networks*. Through the new plugin architecture, various drivers can be provided for different network use cases.

The first of these is the **overlay** driver. In order to coordinate across multiple hosts, they must all agree on the available networks and their topologies. The overlay driver uses a distributed key-value store to synchronize the network creation across multiple hosts.

It's important to note that the plugin mechanism will allow a wide range of networking possibilities in Docker. In fact, many of the third-party options such as Weave are already creating their own Docker network plugins.

# Weave

**Weave** provides an overlay network for Docker containers. It can be used as a plugin with the new Docker network plugin interface, and it is also compatible with Kubernetes. Like many overlay networks, many criticize the performance impact of the encapsulation overhead. Note that they have recently added a preview release with **Virtual Extensible LAN (VXLAN)** encapsulation support, which greatly improves performance. For more information, visit:

```
http://blog.weave.works/2015/06/12/weave-fast-datapath/
```

# Flannel

**Flannel** comes from CoreOS and is an etcd-backed overlay. Flannel gives a full subnet to each host/node enabling a similar pattern to the Kubernetes practice of a routable IP per pod or group of containers. Flannel includes an in-kernel VXLAN encapsulation mode for better performance and has an experimental multinetwork mode similar to the overlay Docker plugin. For more information, visit:

```
https://github.com/coreos/flannel
```

# Project Calico

**Project Calico** is a layer 3-based networking model that uses the built-in routing functions of the Linux kernel. Routes are propagated to virtual routers on each host via **Border Gateway Protocol (BGP)**. Calico can be used for anything from small-scale deploys to large Internet-scale installations. Because it works at a lower level on the network stack, there is no need for additional NAT, tunneling, or overlays. It can interact directly with the underlying network infrastructure. Additionally, it has a support for network-level ACLs to provide additional isolation and security. For more information visit:

```
http://www.projectcalico.org/
```

# Balanced design

It's important to point out the balance Kubernetes is trying to achieve by placing the IP at the pod level. Using unique IP addresses at the host level is problematic as the number of containers grow. Ports must be used to expose services on specific containers and allow external communication. In addition to this, the complexity of running multiple services that may or may not know about each other (and their custom ports), and managing the port space becomes a big issue.

However, assigning an IP address to each container can be overkill. In cases of sizable scale, overlay networks and NATs are needed in order to address each container. Overlay networks add latency, and IP addresses would be taken up by backend services as well since they need to communicate with their frontend counterparts.

Here, we really see an advantage in the abstractions that Kubernetes provides at the application and service level. If I have a web server and a database, we can keep them on the same pod and use a single IP address. The web server and database can use the local interface and standard ports to communicate, and no custom setup is required. Further, services on the backend are not needlessly exposed to other application stacks running elsewhere in the cluster (but possibly on the same host). Since the pod sees the same IP address that the applications running within it see, service discovery does not require any additional translation.

If you need the flexibility of an overlay network, you can still use an overlay at the pod level. Both Weave and Flannel overlays, as well as the BGP routing Project Calico, can be used with Kubernetes.

This is also very helpful in the context of scheduling the workloads. It is a key to have a simple and standard structure for the scheduler to match constraints and understand where space exists on the cluster's network at any given time. This is a dynamic environment with a variety of applications and tasks running, so any additional complexity here will have rippling effects.

There are also implications for service discovery. New services coming online must determine and register an IP address on which the rest of the world, or at least cluster, can reach them. If NAT is used, the services will need an additional mechanism to learn their externally facing IP.

# Advanced services

Let's explore the IP strategy as it relates to Services and communication between containers. If you recall, in *Chapter 2, Kubernetes – Core Concepts and Constructs*, under the *Services* section, you learned that Kubernetes is using kube-proxy to determine the proper pod IP address and port serving each request. Behind the scenes, kube-proxy is actually using virtual IPs and **iptables** to make all this magic work.

Recall that kube-proxy is running on every host. Its first duty is to monitor the API from the Kubernetes master. Any updates to services will trigger an update to iptables from kube-proxy. For example, when a new service is created, a virtual IP address is chosen and a rule in iptables is set, which will direct its traffic to kube-proxy via a random port. Thus, we now have a way to capture service-destined traffic on this node. Since kube-proxy is running on all nodes, we have cluster-wide resolution for the service VIP. Additionally, DNS records can point to this virtual IP as well.

Now that we have a *hook* created in iptables, we still need to get the traffic to the servicing pods; however, the rule is only sending traffic to the service entry in kube-proxy at this point. Once kube-proxy receives the traffic for a particular service, it must then forward it to a pod in the service's pool of candidates. It does this using a random port that was selected during service creation. Refer to the following figure (Figure 3.1) for an overview of the flow:

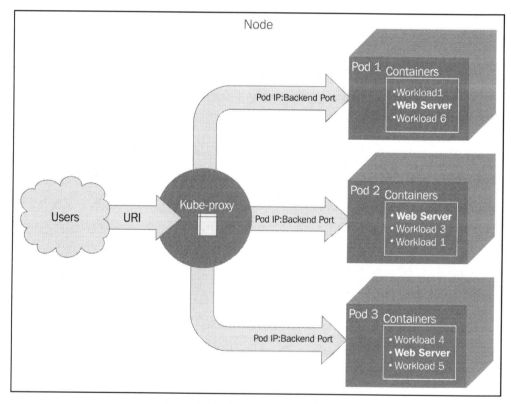

Figure 3.1. Kube-proxy communication

At the time of writing this book, there are plans in the upcoming version 1.1 to include a kube-proxy, which does not rely on service entry and uses only iptable rules.

 It is also possible to always forward traffic from the same client IP to same backend pod/container using the `sessionAffinity` element in your service definition.

# External services

In the last chapter, we saw a few service examples. For testing and demonstration purposes, we wanted all the services to be externally accessible. This was configured by the `type: LoadBalancer` element in our service definition. The `LoadBalancer` type creates an external load balancer on the cloud provider. We should note that support for external load balancers varies by provider as does the implementation. In our case, we are using GCE, so integration is pretty smooth. The only additional setup needed is to open firewall rules for the external service ports.

Let's dig a little deeper and do a `describe` on one of the services from the *Chapter 2, Kubernetes – Core Concepts and Constructs*, under the *More on labels* section.

```
$ kubectl describe service/node-js-labels
```

The following screenshot is the result of the preceding command:

```
Name:                   node-js-labels
Namespace:              default
Labels:                 app=node-js-express,deployment=test,name=node-js-labels
Selector:               app=node-js-express,name=node-js-labels
Type:                   LoadBalancer
IP:                     10.0.115.200
LoadBalancer Ingress:   146.148.56.25
Port:                   <unnamed>        80/TCP
NodePort:               <unnamed>        30237/TCP
Endpoints:              10.244.0.29:80,10.244.2.34:80,10.244.2.35:80
Session Affinity:       None
No events.
```

Figure 3.2. Service description

In the output, in Figure 3.2, you'll note several key elements. Our namespace is set to default, **Type:** is `LoadBalancer`, and we have the external IP listed under **LoadBalancer Ingress:**. Further, we see **Endpoints:**, which shows us the IPs of the pods available to answer service requests.

# Internal services

Let's explore the other types of services we can deploy. First, by default, services are internally facing only. You can specify a type of `clusterIP` to achieve this, but if no type is defined, `clusterIP` is the assumed type. Let's take a look at an example, note the lack of the `type` element:

```
apiVersion: v1
kind: Service
metadata:
  name: node-js-internal
  labels:
    name: node-js-internal
spec:
  ports:
  - port: 80
  selector:
    name: node-js
```

*Listing 3-1*: `nodejs-service-internal.yaml`

Use this listing to create the service definition file. You'll need a healthy version of the `node-js` RC (*Listing 2-7*: `nodejs-health-controller-2.yaml`). As you can see, the selector matches on the pods named `node-js` that our RC launched in the last chapter. We will create the service and then list the currently running services with a filter:

```
$ kubectl create -f nodejs-service-internal.yaml
$ kubectl get services -l name=node-js-internal
```

The following screenshot is the result of the preceding command:

| NAME | LABELS | SELECTOR | IP(S) | PORT(S) |
|------|--------|----------|-------|---------|
| node-js-internal | name=node-js-internal | name=node-js | 10.0.5.134 | 80/TCP |

Figure 3.3. Internal service listing

As you can see, we have a new service, but only one IP. Further, the IP address is not externally accessible. We won't be able to test the service from a web browser this time. However, we can use the handy `kubectl exec` command and attempt to connect from one of the other pods. You will need `node-js-pod` (*Listing 2-1*: `nodejs-pod.yaml`) running. Then, you can execute the following command:

```
$ kubectl exec node-js-pod -- curl <node-js-internal IP>
```

This allows us to run a `docker exec` command as if we had a shell in the `node-js-`pod container. It then hits the internal service URL, which forwards to any pods with the `node-js` label.

If all is well, you should get the raw HTML output back. So, you've successfully created an internal-only service. This can be useful for backend services that you want to make available to other containers running in your cluster, but not open to the world at large.

# Custom load balancing

A third type of service K8s allows is the `NodePort` type. This type allows us to expose a service through the host or minion on a specific port. In this way, we can use the IP address of any node (minion) and access our service on the assigned node port. Kubernetes will assign a node port by default in the range of 3000–32767, but you can also specify your own custom port. In the example in *Listing 3-2*: `nodejs-service-nodeport.yaml`, we choose port `30001` as follows:

```
apiVersion: v1
kind: Service
metadata:
  name: node-js-nodeport
  labels:
    name: node-js-nodeport
spec:
  ports:
  - port: 80
    nodeport: 30001
  selector:
    name: node-js
  type: NodePort
```

*Listing 3-2*: `nodejs-service-nodeport.yaml`

Once again, create this YAML definition file and create your service as follows:

```
$ kubectl create -f nodejs-service-nodeport.yaml
```

The output should have a message like this:

```
You have exposed your service on an external port on all nodes in your
cluster.  If you want to expose this service to the external internet,
you may
need to set up firewall rules for the service port(s) (tcp:30001) to se
rve traffic.

See http://releases.k8s.io/HEAD/docs/user-guide/services-firewalls.md f
or more details.
services/node-js-nodeport
```

Figure 3.4. New GCP firewall rule

You'll note a message about opening firewall ports. Similar to the external load balancer type, `NodePort` is exposing your service externally using ports on the nodes. This could be useful if, for example, you want to use your own load balancer in front of the nodes. Let's make sure that we open those ports on GCP before we test our new service.

From the GCE VM instance console, click on the network for any of your nodes (minions). In my case, it was default. Under firewall rules, we can add a rule by clicking **Add firewall rule**. Create a rule like the one shown in Figure 3.5:

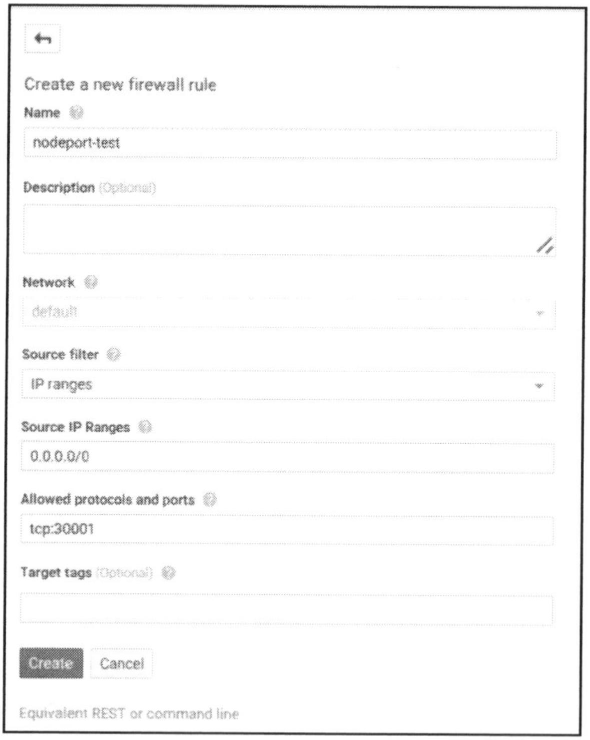

Figure 3.5. New GCP firewall rule

We can now test our new service out, by opening a browser and using an IP address of any node (minion) in your cluster. The format to test the new service is:

```
http://<Minoion IP Address>:<NodePort>/
```

# Cross-node proxy

Remember that kube-proxy is running on all the nodes, so even if the pod is not running there, traffic will be given a proxy to the appropriate host. Refer to Figure 3.6 for a visual on how the traffic flows. A user makes a request to an external IP or URL. The request is serviced by **Node 1** in this case. However, the pod does not happen to run on this node. This is not a problem because the pod IP addresses are routable. So, **Kube-proxy** simply passes traffic on to the pod IP for this service. The network routing then completes on **Node 2**, where the requested application lives.

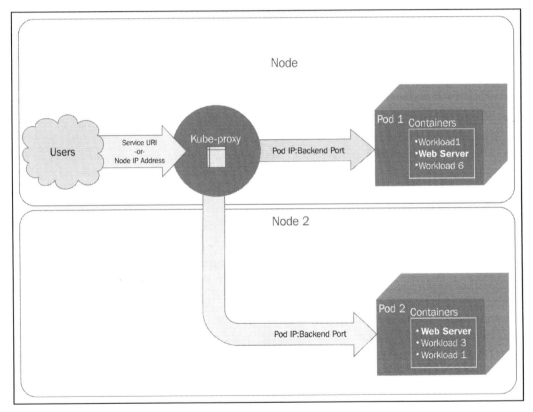

Figure 3.6. Cross-node traffic

# Custom ports

Services also allow you to map your traffic to different ports, then the containers and pods themselves expose. We will create a service that exposes `port 90` and forwards traffic to `port 80` on the pods. We will call the `node-js-90` pod to reflect the custom port number. Create the following two definition files:

```yaml
apiVersion: v1
kind: ReplicationController
metadata:
  name: node-js-90
  labels:
    name: node-js-90
spec:
  replicas: 3
  selector:
    name: node-js-90
  template:
    metadata:
      labels:
        name: node-js-90
    spec:
      containers:
      - name: node-js-90
        image: jonbaier/node-express-info:latest
        ports:
        - containerPort: 80
```

*Listing 3-3*: `nodejs-customPort-controller.yaml`

```yaml
apiVersion: v1
kind: Service
metadata:
  name: node-js-90
  labels:
    name: node-js-90
spec:
  type: LoadBalancer
  ports:
  - port: 90
    targetPort: 80
  selector:
    name: node-js-90
```

*Listing 3-4*: `nodejs-customPort-service.yaml`

You'll note that in the service definition, we have a `targetPort` element. This element tells the service the port to use for pods/containers in the pool. As we saw in previous examples, if you do not specify `targetPort`, it assumes that it's the same port as the service. Port is still used as the service port, but in this case, we are going to expose the service on port `90` while the containers serve content on port `80`.

Create this RC and service and open the appropriate firewall rules, as we did in the last example. It may take a moment for the external load balancer IP to propagate to the `get service` command. Once it does, you should be able to open and see our familiar web application in a browser using the following format:

```
http://<external service IP>:90/
```

# Multiple ports

Another custom port use case is that of multiple ports. Many applications expose multiple ports, such as HTTP on port `80` and port `8888` for web servers. The following example shows our app responding on both ports. Once again, we'll also need to add a firewall rule for this port, as we did for *Listing 3-2*: `nodejs-service-nodeport.yaml` previously:

```yaml
apiVersion: v1
kind: ReplicationController
metadata:
  name: node-js-multi
  labels:
    name: node-js-multi
spec:
  replicas: 3
  selector:
    name: node-js-multi
  template:
    metadata:
      labels:
        name: node-js-multi
    spec:
      containers:
      - name: node-js-multi
        image: jonbaier/node-express-multi:latest
        ports:
        - containerPort: 80
        - containerPort: 8888
```

*Listing 3-5:* `nodejs-multicontroller.yaml`

```
apiVersion: v1
kind: Service
metadata:
  name: node-js-multi
  labels:
    name: node-js-multi
spec:
  type: LoadBalancer
  ports:
  - name: http
    protocol: TCP
    port: 80
  - name: fake-admin-http
    protocol: TCP
    port: 8888
  selector:
    name: node-js-multi
```

*Listing 3-6:* `nodejs-multiservice.yaml`

Note that the application and container itself must be listening on both ports for this to work. In this example, port `8888` is used to represent a fake admin interface.

If, for example, you want to listen on port 443, you would need a proper SSL socket listening on the server.

# Migrations, multicluster, and more

As you've seen so far, Kubernetes offers a high level of flexibility and customization to create a service abstraction around your containers running in the cluster. However, there may be times where you want to point to something outside your cluster.

An example of this would be working with legacy systems, or even applications running on another cluster. In the case of the former, this is a perfectly good strategy in order to migrate to Kubernetes and containers in general. We can begin to manage the service endpoints in Kubernetes while stitching the stack together using the K8s orchestration concepts. Additionally, we can even start bringing over pieces of the stack, as the frontend, one at a time as the organization refactors applications for microservices and/or containerization.

To allow access to non-pod–based applications, the services construct allows you to use endpoints that are outside the cluster. Kubernetes is actually creating an endpoint resource every time you create a service that uses selectors. The `endpoints` object keeps track of the pod IPs in the load balancing pool. You can see this by running a `get endpoints` command as follows:

```
$ kubectl get endpoints
```

You should see something similar to this:

```
NAME                ENDPOINTS
http-pd             10.244.2.29:80,10.244.2.30:80,10.244.3.16:80
kubernetes          10.240.0.2:443
node-js             10.244.0.12:80,10.244.2.24:80,10.244.3.13:80
```

You'll note an entry for all the services we currently have running on our cluster. For most, the endpoints are just the IP of each pod running in a RC. As I mentioned, Kubernetes does this automatically based on the selector. As we scale the replicas in a controller with matching labels, Kubernetes will update the endpoints automatically.

If we want to create a service for something that is not a pod and therefore has no labels to select, we can easily do this with both a service and endpoint definition as follows:

```
apiVersion: v1
kind: Service
metadata:
  name: custom-service
spec:
  type: LoadBalancer
  ports:
  - name: http
    protocol: TCP
    port: 80
```

*Listing 3-7*: `nodejs-custom-service.yaml`

```
apiVersion: v1
kind: Endpoints
metadata:
  name: custom-service
subsets:
- addresses:
  - IP: <X.X.X.X>
  ports:
```

```
  - name: http
    port: 80
    protocol: TCP
```

*Listing 3-8*: `nodejs-custom-endpoint.yaml`

In the preceding example, you'll need to replace the `<X.X.X.X>` with a real IP address where the new service can point. In my case, I used the public load balancer IP from `node-js-multiservice` we created earlier. Go ahead and create these resources now.

If we now run a `get endpoints` command, we will see this IP address at port `80` associated with the `custom-service` endpoint. Further, if we look at the service details, we will see the IP listed in the `Endpoints` section.

```
$ kubectl describe service/custom-service
```

We can test out this new service by opening the `custom-service` external IP from a browser.

# Custom addressing

Another option to customize services is with the `clusterIP` element. In our examples this far, we've not specified an IP address, which means that it chooses the internal address of the service for us. However, we can add this element and choose the IP address in advance with something like `clusterip: 10.0.125.105`.

There may be times when you don't want to load balance and would rather have DNS with *A* records for each pod. For example, software that needs to replicate data evenly to all nodes may rely on *A* records to distribute data. In this case, we can use an example like the following one and set `clusterip` to `None`. Kubernetes will not assign an IP address and instead only assign *A* records in DNS for each of the pods. If you are using DNS, the service should be available at `node-js-none` or `node-js-none.default.cluster.local` from within the cluster. We have the following code:

```
apiVersion: v1
kind: Service
metadata:
  name: node-js-none
  labels:
    name: node-js-none
spec:
  clusterip: None
  ports:
  - port: 80
  selector:
    name: node-js
```

*Listing 3-9*: `nodejs-headless-service.yaml`

Test it out after you create this service with the trusty `exec` command:

```
$ kubectl exec node-js-pod -- curl node-js-none
```

# Service discovery

As we discussed earlier, the Kubernetes master keeps track of all service definitions and updates. Discovery can occur in one of three ways. The first two methods use Linux environment variables. There is support for the Docker link style of environment variables, but Kubernetes also has its own naming convention. Here is an example of what our `node-js` service example might look like using K8s environment variables (note IPs will vary):

```
NODE_JS_PORT_80_TCP=tcp://10.0.103.215:80
NODE_JS_PORT=tcp://10.0.103.215:80
NODE_JS_PORT_80_TCP_PROTO=tcp
NODE_JS_PORT_80_TCP_PORT=80
NODE_JS_SERVICE_HOST=10.0.103.215
NODE_JS_PORT_80_TCP_ADDR=10.0.103.215
NODE_JS_SERVICE_PORT=80
```

*Listing 3-10*: *Service environment variables*

Another option for discovery is through DNS. While environment variables can be useful when DNS is not available, it has drawbacks. The system only creates variables at creation time, so services that come online later will not be discovered or would require some additional tooling to update all the system environments.

# DNS

DNS solves the issues seen with environment variables by allowing us to reference the services by their name. As services restart, scale out, or appear anew, the DNS entries will be updating and ensuring that the service name always points to the latest infrastructure. DNS is set up by default in most of the supported providers.

If DNS is supported by your provider, but not setup, you can configure the following variables in your default provider `config` when you create your Kubernetes cluster:

```
ENABLE_CLUSTER_DNS="${KUBE_ENABLE_CLUSTER_DNS:-true}"
DNS_SERVER_IP="10.0.0.10"
DNS_DOMAIN="cluster.local"
DNS_REPLICAS=1
```

With DNS active, services can be accessed in one of two forms—either the service name itself, `<service-name>`, or a fully qualified name that includes the namespace, `<service-name>.<namespace-name>.cluster.local`. In our examples, it would look similar to `node-js-90` or `node-js-90.default.cluster.local`.

# Persistent storage

Let's switch gears for a moment and talk about another core concept: persistent storage. When you start moving from development to production, one of the most obvious challenges you face is the transient nature of containers themselves. If you recall our discussion of layered file systems in *Chapter 1, Kubernetes and Container Operations*, the top layer is writable. (It's also frosting, which is delicious.) However, when the container dies, the data goes with it. The same is true for crashed containers that Kubernetes restarts.

This is where **persistent disks (PDs)**, or volumes, come into play. A persistent volume that exists outside the container allows us to save our important data across containers outages. Further, if we have a volume at the pod level, data can be shared between containers in the same application stack and within the same pod.

Docker itself has some support for volumes, but Kubernetes gives us persistent storage that lasts beyond the lifetime of a single container. The volumes are tied to pods and live and die with those pods. Additionally, a pod can have multiple volumes from a variety of sources. Let's take a look at some of these sources.

# Temporary disks

One of the easiest ways to achieve improved persistence amid container crashes and data sharing within a pod is to use the `emptydir` volume. This volume type can be used with either the storage volumes of the node machine itself or an optional RAM disk for higher performance.

Again, we improve our persistence beyond a single container, but when a pod is removed, the data will be lost. Machine reboot will also clear any data from RAM-type disks. There may be times when we just need some shared temporary space or have containers that process data and hand it off to another container before they die. Whatever the case, here is a quick example of using this temporary disk with the RAM-backed option.

Open your favorite editor and create a file like the one in *Listing 3-11*:
`storage-memory.yaml` here:

```
apiVersion: v1
kind: Pod
metadata:
  name: memory-pd
spec:
  containers:
  - image: nginx:latest
    ports:
    - containerPort: 80
    name: memory-pd
    volumeMounts:
    - mountPath: /memory-pd
      name: memory-volume
  volumes:
  - name: memory-volume
    emptydir:
      medium: Memory
```

*Listing 3-11*: `storage-memory.yaml`

It's probably second nature by now, but we will once again issue a `create` command
followed by an `exec` command to see the folders in the container:

```
$ kubectl create -f storage-memory.yaml
$ kubectl exec memory-pd -- ls -lh | grep memory-pd
```

This will give us a bash shell in the container itself. The `ls` command shows us a
`memory-pd` folder at the top level. We use `grep` to filter the output, but you can run
the command without | `grep memory-pd` to see all folders.

```
/home/k8s/nodejs# kubectl.sh exec memory-pd -- ls -lh | grep memory
drwxrwxrwt  2 root root    40 Oct 24 15:21 memory-pd
```

Figure 3.7. Temporary storage inside a container

Again, this folder is quite temporary as everything is stored in the minion's RAM.
When the node gets restarted, all the files will be erased. We will look at a more
permanent example next.

# Cloud volumes

Many companies will already have significant infrastructure running in the public cloud. Luckily, Kubernetes has native support for the persistent volume types provided by two of the most popular providers.

## GCE persistent disks

Let's create a new **GCE persistent volume**. From the console, under **Compute**, go to **Disks**. On this new screen, click on the **New disk** button.

We'll be presented with a screen similar to Figure 3.8. Choose a name for this volume and give it a brief description. Make sure that the zone is the same as the nodes in your cluster. GCE PDs can only be attached to machines in the same zone.

Enter `mysite-volume-1` for the **Name**. Choose a **Source type** of **None (blank disk)** and give `10` (10 GB) as value in **Size (GB)**. Finally, click on **Create**.

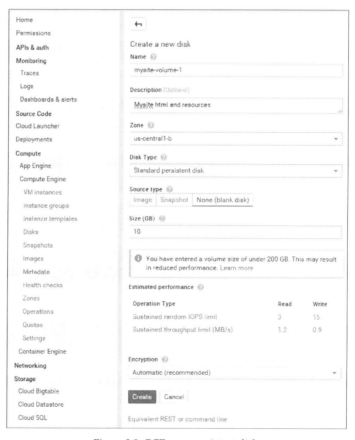

Figure 3.8. GCE new persistent disk

The nice thing about PDs on GCE is that they allow for mounting to multiple machines (nodes in our case). However, when mounting to multiple machines, the volume must be in read-only mode. So, let's first mount this to a single pod, so we can create some files. Use *Listing 3-12*: `storage-gce.yaml` as follows to create a pod that will mount the disk in read/write mode:

```
apiVersion: v1
kind: Pod
metadata:
  name: test-gce
spec:
  containers:
  - image: nginx:latest
    ports:
    - containerPort: 80
    name: test-gce
    volumeMounts:
    - mountPath: /usr/share/nginx/html
      name: gce-pd
  volumes:
  - name: gce-pd
    gcePersistentDisk:
      pdName: mysite-volume-1
      fsType: ext4
```

*Listing 3-12*: `storage-gce.yaml`

First, let's issue a `create` command followed by a describe to find out which node it is running on. Note the node and save the pod IP address for later. Then, open an SSH session into the node.

```
$ kubectl create -f storage-gce.yaml

$ kubectl describe pod/test-gce

$ gcloud compute --project "<Your project ID>" ssh --zone "<your gce
zone>" "<Node running test-gce pod>"
```

Since we've already looked at the volume from inside the running container, let's access it directly from the minion node itself this time. We will run a `df` command to see where it is mounted:

```
$ df -h | grep mysite-volume-1
```

As you can see, the GCE volume is mounted directly to the node itself. We can use the mount path listed in the output of the earlier `df` command. Use `cd` to change to the folder now. Then, create a new file named `index.html` with your favorite editor:

```
$ cd /var/lib/kubelet/plugins/kubernetes.io/gce-pd/mounts/mysite-volume-1
$ vi index.html
```

Enter a quaint message such as `Hello from my GCE PD!`. Now save the file and exit the editor. If you recall from *Listing 3-12*: `storage-gce.yaml`, the PD is mounted directly to the NGINX html directory. So, let's test this out while we still have the SSH session open on the node. Do a simple `curl` command to the pod IP we wrote down earlier.

```
$ curl <Pod IP from Describe>
```

You should see **Hello from my GCE PD!** or whatever message you saved in the `index.html` file. In a real-world scenario, we could use the volume for an entire website or any other central storage. Let's take a look at running a set of load balanced web servers all pointing to the same volume.

First, leave the SSH session with `exit`. Before we proceed, we will need to remove our `test-gce` pod so that the volume can be mounted read-only across a number of nodes.

```
$ kubectl delete pod/test-gce
```

Now we can create a RC that will run three web servers all mounting the same persistent volume as follows:

```
apiVersion: v1
kind: ReplicationController
metadata:
  name: http-pd
  labels:
    name: http-pd
spec:
  replicas: 3
  selector:
    name: http-pd
  template:
    metadata:
      name: http-pd
    spec:
      containers:
```

```
- image: nginx:latest
  ports:
  - containerPort: 80
  name: http-pd
  volumeMounts:
  - mountPath: /usr/share/nginx/html
    name: gce-pd
volumes:
- name: gce-pd
  gcePersistentDisk:
    pdName: mysite-volume-1
    fsType: ext4
    readOnly: true
```

*Listing 3-13*: `http-pd-controller.yaml`

Let's also create an external service, so we can see it from outside the cluster:

```
apiVersion: v1
kind: Service
metadata:
  name: http-pd
  labels:
    name: http-pd
spec:
  type: LoadBalancer
  ports:
  - name: http
    protocol: TCP
    port: 80
  selector:
    name: http-pd
```

*Listing 3-14*: `http-pd-service.yaml`

Go ahead and create these two resources now. Wait a few moments for the external IP to get assigned. After this, a `describe` command will give us the IP we can use in a browser:

```
$ kubectl describe service/http-pd
```

The following screenshot is the result of the preceding command:

```
Name:                   http-pd
Namespace:              default
Labels:                 name=http-pd
Selector:               name=http-pd
Type:                   LoadBalancer
IP:                     10.0.118.195
LoadBalancer Ingress:   130.211.186.84
Port:                   http    80/TCP
NodePort:               http    32429/TCP
Endpoints:              10.244.2.15:80,10.244.2.16:80,10.244.3.5:80
Session Affinity:       None
No events.
```

Figure 3.9. K8s service with GCE PD shared across three pods

Type the IP address into a browser, and you should see your familiar `index.html` file show up with the text we entered previously!

# AWS Elastic Block Store

K8s also supports AWS **Elastic Block Store (EBS)** volumes. Like the GCE PDs, EBS volumes are required to be attached to an instance running in the same availability zone. A further limitation is that EBS can only be mounted to a single instance at one time.

For brevity, we will not walk through an AWS example, but a sample YAML file is included to get you started. Again, remember to create the EBS volume before your pod.

```
apiVersion: v1
kind: Pod
metadata:
  name: test-aws
spec:
  containers:
  - image: nginx:latest
    ports:
    - containerPort: 80
    name: test-aws
    volumeMounts:
    - mountPath: /usr/share/nginx/html
      name: aws-pd
  volumes:
  - name: aws-pd
    awsElasticBlockStore:
      volumeID: aws://<availability-zone>/<volume-id>
      fsType: ext4
```

*Listing 3-15*: `storage-aws.yaml`

# Other PD options

Kubernetes supports a variety of other types of persistent storage. A full list can be found here:

```
http://kubernetes.io/v1.0/docs/user-guide/volumes.html#types-of-
volumes
```

Here are a few that may be of particular interest:

- `nfs`: This type allows us to mount a **Network File Share (NFS)**, which can be very useful for both persisting the data and sharing it across the infrastructure
- `gitrepo`: As you might have guessed, this option clones a Git repo into an a new and empty folder

# Multitenancy

Kubernetes also has an additional construct for isolation at the cluster level. In most cases, you can run Kubernetes and never worry about namespaces; everything will run in the default namespace if not specified. However, in cases where you run multitenancy communities or want broad-scale segregation and isolation of the cluster resources, namespaces can be used to this end.

To start, Kubernetes has two namespaces: `default` and `kube-system`. `kube-system` is used for all the system-level containers we saw in *Chapter 1, Kubernetes and Container Operations*, under the *Services running on the minions* section. The UI, logging, DNS, and so on are all run under `kube-system`. Everything else the user creates runs in the default namespace. However, our resource definition files can optionally specify a custom namespace. For the sake of experimenting, let's take a look at how to build a new namespace.

First, we'll need to create a namespace definition file like the one in this listing:

```
apiVersion: v1
kind: Namespace
metadata:
  name: test
```

*Listing 3-16*: `test-ns.yaml`

We can go ahead and create this file with our handy `create` command:

```
$ kubectl create -f test-ns.yaml
```

Now we can create resources that use the `test` namespace. The following is an example of a pod using this new namespace. We have the following:

```
apiVersion: v1
kind: Pod
metadata:
  name: utility
  namespace: test
spec:
  containers:
  - image: debian:latest
    command:
      - sleep
      - "3600"
    name: utility
```

*Listing 3-17:* `ns-pod.yaml`

While the pod can still access services in other namespaces, it will need to use the long DNS form of `<service-name>.<namespace-name>.cluster.local`. For example, if you were to run command from inside the container in *Listing 3-17:* `ns-pod.yaml`, you could use `http-pd.default.cluster.local` to access the PD example from *Listing 3-14:* `http-pd-service.yaml`.

# Limits

Let's inspect our new namespace a bit more. Run the `describe` command as follows:

**$ kubectl describe namespace/test**

The following screenshot is the result of the preceding command:

```
Name:    test
Labels:  <none>
Status:  Active

No resource quota.

No resource limits.
```

Figure 3.10. Namespace describe

Kubernetes allows you to both limit the resources used by individual pods or containers and the resources used by the overall namespace using quotas. You'll note that there are no resource **limits** or **quotas** currently set on the test namespace.

Suppose we want to limit the footprint of this new namespace; we can set quotas such as the following:

```
apiVersion: v1
kind: ResourceQuota
metadata:
  name: test-quotas
  namespace: test
spec:
  hard:
    pods: 3
    services: 1
    replicationcontrollers: 1
```

*Listing 3-18*: `quota.yaml`

 Note that in reality, namespaces would be for larger application communities and would probably never have quotas this low. I am using this in order to ease illustration of the capability in the example.

Here, we will create a quota of 3 pods, 1 RC, and 1 service for the test namespace. As you probably guessed, this is executed once again by our trusty `create` command:

**$ kubectl create -f quota.yaml**

Now that we have that in place, let's use `describe` on the namespace as follows:

**$ kubectl describe namespace/test**

The following screenshot is the result of the preceding command:

```
Name:    test
Labels:  <none>
Status:  Active

Resource Quotas
 Resource               Used    Hard
 ---                    ---     ---
 pods                   0       3
 replicationcontrollers 0       1
 services               0       1

No resource limits.
```

Figure 3.11. Namespace describe after quota is set

You'll note that we now have some values listed in the quota section and the limits section is still blank. We also have a **Used** column, which lets us know how close to the limits we are at the moment. Let's try to spin up a few pods using the following definition:

```
apiVersion: v1
kind: ReplicationController
metadata:
  name: busybox-ns
  namespace: test
  labels:
    name: busybox-ns
spec:
  replicas: 4
  selector:
    name: busybox-ns
  template:
    metadata:
      labels:
        name: busybox-ns
    spec:
      containers:
      - name: busybox-ns
        image: busybox
        command:
          - sleep
          - "3600"
```

*Listing 3-19*: `busybox-ns.yaml`

You'll note that we are creating four replicas of this basic pod. After using `create` to build this RC, run the `describe` command on the `test` namespace once more. You'll note that the `used` values for pods and RCs are at their max. However, we asked for four replicas and only see three pods in use.

Let's see what's happening with our RC. You might tempt to do that with the command here:

**kubectl describe rc/busybox-ns**

However, if you try, you'll be disparaged to see a **not found** message from the server. This is because we created this RC in a new namespace and `kubectl` assumes the default namespace if not specified. This means that we need to specify `--namepsace=test` with every command when we wish to access resources in the `test` namespace.

We can also set the current namespace by working with the context settings. First, we need to find our current context, which is found with the following command:

```
$ kubectl config view | grep current-context
```

Next, we can take that context and set the namespace variable like the following:

```
$ kubectl config set-context <Current Context>
--namespace=test
```

Now you can run the kubectl command without the need to specify the namespace. Just remember to switch back when you want to look at the resources running in your default namespace.

Run the command with the namespace specified like so. If you've set your current namespace as demonstrated in the tip box, you can leave off the --namespace argument:

```
$ kubectl describe rc/busybox-ns --namespace=test
```

The following screenshot is the result of the preceding command:

```
Name:               busybox-ns
Namespace:          test
Image(s):           busybox
Selector:           name=busybox-ns
Labels:             name=busybox-ns
Replicas:           3 current / 4 desired
Pods Status:        3 Running / 0 Waiting / 0 Succeeded / 0 Failed
Events:
  FirstSeen                               LastSeen                          Count    F
rom                           SubobjectPath    Reason                       Message
  Mon, 17 Aug 2015 16:29:43 -0400     Mon, 17 Aug 2015 16:29:43 -0400  1            {
replication-controller }                        successfulCreate             Created p
od: busybox-ns-spfrn
  Mon, 17 Aug 2015 16:29:43 -0400     Mon, 17 Aug 2015 16:29:43 -0400  1            {
replication-controller }                        successfulCreate             Created p
od: busybox-ns-xjf6q
  Mon, 17 Aug 2015 16:29:43 -0400     Mon, 17 Aug 2015 16:29:43 -0400  1            {
replication-controller }                        successfulCreate             Created p
od: busybox-ns-zeuuy
  Mon, 17 Aug 2015 16:29:44 -0400     Mon, 17 Aug 2015 16:33:01 -0400  18           {
replication-controller }                        failedCreate                 Error cre
ating: Pod "busybox-ns-" is forbidden: Limited to 3 pods
```

Figure 3.12. Namespace quotas

As you can see in the preceding image, the first three pods were successfully created, but our final one fails with the error **Limited to 3 pods**.

This is an easy way to set limits for resources partitioned out at a community scale. It's worth noting that you can also set quotas for CPU, memory, persistent volumes, and secrets. Additionally, limits work similar to quota, but they set the limit for each pod or container within the namespace.

# Summary

We took a deeper look into networking and services in Kubernetes. You should now understand how networking communications are designed in K8s and feel comfortable accessing your services internally and externally. We saw how kube-proxy balances traffic both locally and across the cluster. We also looked briefly at how DNS and service discovery is achieved in Kubernetes. In the later portion of the chapter, we explored a variety of persistent storage options. We finished off with quick look at namespace and isolation for multitenancy.

# Footnotes

[1]`http://www.wired.com/2015/06/google-reveals-secret-gear-connects-online-empire/`

# 4
# Updates and
# Gradual Rollouts

This chapter will expand upon the core concepts, which show the reader how to roll out updates and test new features of their application with minimal disruption to uptime. It will cover the basics of doing application updates, gradual rollouts, and A/B testing. In addition, we will look at scaling the Kubernetes cluster itself.

This chapter will discuss the following topics:

- Application scaling
- Rolling updates
- A/B testing
- Scaling up your cluster

## Example set up

Before we start exploring the various capabilities built into Kubernetes for scaling and updates, we will need a new example environment. We are going to use a variation of our previous container image with a blue background (refer to Figure 4.2 for a comparison). We have the following code:

```
apiVersion: v1
kind: ReplicationController
metadata:
  name: node-js-scale
  labels:
    name: node-js-scale
spec:
  replicas: 1
```

```
  selector:
    name: node-js-scale
  template:
    metadata:
      labels:
        name: node-js-scale
    spec:
      containers:
      - name: node-js-scale
        image: jonbaier/pod-scaling:0.1
        ports:
        - containerPort: 80
```

*Listing 4-1:* `pod-scaling-controller.yaml`

```
  apiVersion: v1
  kind: Service
  metadata:
    name: node-js-scale
    labels:
      name: node-js-scale
  spec:
    type: LoadBalancer
    sessionAffinity: ClientIP
    ports:
    - port: 80
    selector:
      name: node-js-scale
```

*Listing 4-2:* `pod-scaling-service.yaml`

Create these services with the following commands:

```
$ kubectl create -f pod-scaling-controller.yaml
$ kubectl create -f pod-scaling-service.yaml
```

# Scaling up

Over time, as you run your applications in the Kubernetes cluster, you will find that some applications need more resources, whereas others can manage with fewer resources. Instead of removing the entire RC (and associated pods), we want a more seamless way to scale our application up and down.

Thankfully, Kubernetes includes a `scale` command, which is suited specifically to this purpose. In our new example, we have only one replica running. You can check this with a `get pods` command.

```
$ kubectl get pods -l name=node-js-scale
```

Let's try scaling that up to three with the following command:

```
$ kubectl scale --replicas=3 rc/node-js-scale
```

If all goes well, you'll simply see the word **scaled** on the output of your terminal window.

 Optionally, you can specify the `--current-replicas` flag as a verification step. The scaling will only occur if the actual number of replicas currently running matches this count.

After listing our pods once again, we should now see three pods running with a name similar to `node-js-scale-`**xxxxx**, where the xs are a random string.

You can also use the `scale` command to reduce the number of replicas. In either case, the `scale` command adds or removes the necessary pod replicas, and the service automatically updates and balances across new or remaining replicas.

# Smooth updates

The scaling of our application up and down as our resource demands change is useful for many production scenarios, but what about simple application updates? Any production system will have code updates, patches, and feature additions. These could be occurring monthly, weekly, or even daily. Making sure that we have a reliable way to push out these changes without interruption to our users is a paramount consideration.

Once again, we benefit from the years of experience the Kubernetes system is built on. There is a built-in support for rolling updates with the 1.0 version. The `rolling-update` command allows us to update entire RCs or just the underlying Docker image used by each replica. We can also specify an update interval, which will allow us to update one pod at a time and wait until proceeding to the next.

Let's take our scaling example and perform a rolling update to the 0.2 version of our container image. We will use an update interval of 2 minutes, so we can watch the process as it happens in the following way:

```
$ kubectl rolling-update node-js-scale --image=jonbaier/pod-scaling:0.2
--update-period="2m"
```

You should see some text about creating a new RC named node-js-scale-XXXXX, where the xs will be a random string of numbers and letters. In addition, you will see the beginning of a loop that is starting one replica of the new version and removing one from the existing RC. This process will continue until the new RC has the full count of replicas running.

If we want to follow along in real time, we can open another terminal window and use the get pods command, along with a label filter, to see what's happening.

```
$ kubectl get pods -l name=node-js-scale
```

This command will filter for pods with node-js-scale in the name. If you run this after issuing the rolling-update command, you should see several pods running as it creates new versions and removes the old ones one by one.

The full output of the previous rolling-update command should look something like Figure 4.1, as follows:

```
Creating node-js-scale-10ea08ff9a118ac6a93f85547ed2d8f6
At beginning of loop: node-js-scale replicas: 2, node-js-scale-10ea08ff9a118ac6a
93f85547ed2d8f6 replicas: 1
Updating node-js-scale replicas: 2, node-js-scale-10ea08ff9a118ac6a93f85547ed2d8
f6 replicas: 1
At end of loop: node-js-scale replicas: 2, node-js-scale-10ea08ff9a118ac6a93f855
47ed2d8f6 replicas: 1
At beginning of loop: node-js-scale replicas: 1, node-js-scale-10ea08ff9a118ac6a
93f85547ed2d8f6 replicas: 2
Updating node-js-scale replicas: 1, node-js-scale-10ea08ff9a118ac6a93f85547ed2d8
f6 replicas: 2
At end of loop: node-js-scale replicas: 1, node-js-scale-10ea08ff9a118ac6a93f855
47ed2d8f6 replicas: 2
At beginning of loop: node-js-scale replicas: 0, node-js-scale-10ea08ff9a118ac6a
93f85547ed2d8f6 replicas: 3
Updating node-js-scale replicas: 0, node-js-scale-10ea08ff9a118ac6a93f85547ed2d8
f6 replicas: 3
At end of loop: node-js-scale replicas: 0, node-js-scale-10ea08ff9a118ac6a93f855
47ed2d8f6 replicas: 3
Update succeeded. Deleting old controller: node-js-scale
Renaming node-js-scale-10ea08ff9a118ac6a93f85547ed2d8f6 to node-js-scale
node-js-scale
```

Figure 4.1. The scaling output

As we can see here, Kubernetes is first creating a new RC named node-js-scale-10ea08ff9a118ac6a93f85547ed28f6. K8s then loops through one by one. Creating a new pod in the new controller and removing one from the old. This continues until the new controller has the full replica count and the old one is at zero. After this, the old controller is deleted and the new one is renamed to the original controller name.

If you run a `get pods` command now, you'll note that the pods still all have a longer name. Alternatively, we could have specified the name of a new controller in the command, and Kubernetes will create a new RC and pods using that name. Once again, the controller of the old name simply disappears after updating is complete. I recommend specifying a new name for the updated controller to avoid confusion in your pod naming down the line. The same `update` command with this method would look like this:

```
$ kubectl rolling-update node-js-scale node-js-scale-v2.0
--image=jonbaier/pod-scaling:0.2 --update-period="2m"
```

Using the static external IP address from the service we created in the first section, we can open the service in a browser. We should see our standard container information page. However, you'll note that the title now says **Pod Scaling v0.2** and the background is light yellow.

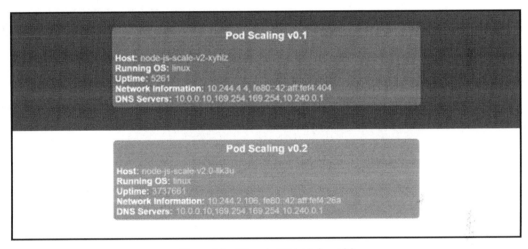

Figure 4.2. v0.1 and v0.2 (side by side)

It's worth noting that during the entire update process, we've only been looking at pods and RCs. We didn't do anything with our service, but the service is still running fine and now directing to the new version of our pods. This is because our service is using label selectors for membership. Because both our old and new replicas use the same labels, the service has no problem using the new pods to service requests. The updates are done on the pods one by one, so it's seamless for the users of the service.

# Testing, releases, and cutovers

The rolling update feature can work well for a simple blue-green deployment scenario. However, in a real-world blue-green deployment with a stack of multiple applications, there can be a variety of interdependencies that require in-depth testing. The `update-period` command allows us to add a `timeout` flag where some testing can be done, but this will not always be satisfactory for testing purposes.

Similarly, you may want partial changes to persist for a longer time and all the way up to the load balancer or service level. For example, you wish to A/B test a new user interface feature with a portion of your users. Another example is running a canary release (a replica in this case) of your application on new infrastructure like a newly added cluster node.

Let's take a look at an A/B testing example. For this example, we will need to create a new service that uses `sessionAffinity`. We will set the affinity to `ClientIP`, which will allow us to forward clients to the same backend pod. This is a key if we want a portion of our users to see one version while others see another:

```
apiVersion: v1
kind: Service
metadata:
  name: node-js-scale-ab
  labels:
    service: node-js-scale-ab
spec:
  type: LoadBalancer
  ports:
  - port: 80
  sessionAffinity: ClientIP
  selector:
    service: node-js-scale-ab
```

*Listing 4-3*: `pod-AB-service.yaml`

Create this service as usual with the `create` command as follows:

```
$ kubectl create -f pod-AB-service.yaml
```

This will create a service that will point to our pods running both version 0.2 and 0.3 of the application. Next, we will create the two RCs which create two replicas of the application. One set will have version 0.2 of the application, and the other will have version 0.3, as shown here:

```
apiVersion: v1
kind: ReplicationController
metadata:
  name: node-js-scale-a
  labels:
    name: node-js-scale-a
    version: "0.2"
    service: node-js-scale-ab
spec:
  replicas: 2
  selector:
    name: node-js-scale-a
    version: "0.2"
    service: node-js-scale-ab
  template:
    metadata:
      labels:
        name: node-js-scale-a
        version: "0.2"
        service: node-js-scale-ab
    spec:
      containers:
      - name: node-js-scale
        image: jonbaier/pod-scaling:0.2
        ports:
        - containerPort: 80
        livenessProbe:
          # An HTTP health check
          httpGet:
            path: /
            port: 80
          initialDelaySeconds: 30
          timeoutSeconds: 5
        readinessProbe:
          # An HTTP health check
          httpGet:
            path: /
            port: 80
          initialDelaySeconds: 30
          timeoutSeconds: 1
```

*Listing 4-4:* `pod-A-controller.yaml`

```yaml
apiVersion: v1
kind: ReplicationController
metadata:
  name: node-js-scale-b
  labels:
    name: node-js-scale-b
    version: "0.3"
    service: node-js-scale-ab
spec:
  replicas: 2
  selector:
    name: node-js-scale-b
    version: "0.3"
    service: node-js-scale-ab
  template:
    metadata:
      labels:
        name: node-js-scale-b
        version: "0.3"
        service: node-js-scale-ab
    spec:
      containers:
      - name: node-js-scale
        image: jonbaier/pod-scaling:0.3
        ports:
        - containerPort: 80
        livenessProbe:
          # An HTTP health check
          httpGet:
            path: /
            port: 80
          initialDelaySeconds: 30
          timeoutSeconds: 5
        readinessProbe:
          # An HTTP health check
          httpGet:
            path: /
            port: 80
          initialDelaySeconds: 30
          timeoutSeconds: 1
```

*Listing 4-5:* `pod-B-controller.yaml`

Note that we have the same service label, so these replicas will also be added to the service pool based on this selector. We also have `livenessProbe` and `readinessProbe` defined to make sure that our new version is working as expected. Again, use the `create` command to spin up the controller:

```
$ kubectl create -f pod-A-controller.yaml
$ kubectl create -f pod-B-controller.yaml
```

Now we have a service balancing to both versions of our app. In a true A/B test, we would now want to start collecting metrics on the visit to each version. Again, we have the `sessionAffinity` set to `ClientIP`, so all requests will go to the same pod. Some users will see v0.2, and some will see v0.3.

 Because we have `sessionAffinity` turned on, your test will likely show the same version every time. This is expected, and you would need to attempt a connection from multiple IP addresses to see both user experiences with each version.

Since the versions are each on their own pod, one can easily separate logging and even add a logging container to the pod definition for a sidecar logging pattern. For brevity, we will not cover that setup in this book, but we will look at some of the logging tools in *Chapter 6, Monitoring and Logging*.

We can start to see how this process would be useful for a canary release or a manual blue-green deployment. We can also see how easy it is to launch a new version and slowly transition over to the new release.

Let's look at a basic transition quickly. It's really as simple as a few `scale` commands, which are as follows:

```
$ kubectl scale --replicas=3 rc/node-js-scale-b
$ kubectl scale --replicas=1 rc/node-js-scale-a
$ kubectl scale --replicas=4 rc/node-js-scale-b
$ kubectl scale --replicas=0 rc/node-js-scale-a
```

 Use the `get pods` command combined with `-l` filter in between `scale` commands to watch the transition as it happens.

Now we have fully transitioned over to version 0.3 (node-js-scale-b). All users will now see the version 0.3 of the site. We have four replicas of version 0.3 and 0 of 0.2. If you run a get rc command, you will notice that we still have a RC for 0.2 (node-js-scale-a). As a final cleanup, we can remove that controller completely as follows:

```
$ kubectl delete rc/node-js-scale-a
```

> In the newly released version 1.1, K8s has a new "Horizontal Pod Autoscaler" construct which allows you to automatically scale pods based on CPU utilization.

# Growing your cluster

All these techniques are great for the scaling of the application, but what about the cluster itself. At some point, you will pack the nodes full and need more resources to schedule new pods for your workloads.

> When you create your cluster, you can customize the starting number of (minions) nodes with the NUM_MINIONS environment variable. By default, it is set to 4. The following example shows how to set it to 5 before running kube-up.sh:
>
> ```
> $ export NUM_MINIONS = 5
> ```
>
> Bear in mind that changing this after the cluster is started will have no effect. You would need to tear down the cluster and create it once again. Thus, this section will show you how to add nodes to an existing cluster without rebuilding it.

# Scaling up the cluster on GCE

Scaling up your cluster on GCE is actually quite easy. The existing plumbing uses managed instance groups in GCE, which allow you to easily add more machines of a standard configuration to the group via an instance template.

You can see this template easily in the GCE console. First, open the console; by default, this should open your default project console. If you are using another project for your Kubernetes cluster, simply select it from the project dropdown at the top of the page.

On the side panel under **Compute** and then **Compute Engine**, select **Instance templates**. You should see a template titled **kuberenetes-minion-template**. Note that the name could vary slightly if you've customized your cluster naming settings. Click on that template to see the details. Refer to the following screenshot:

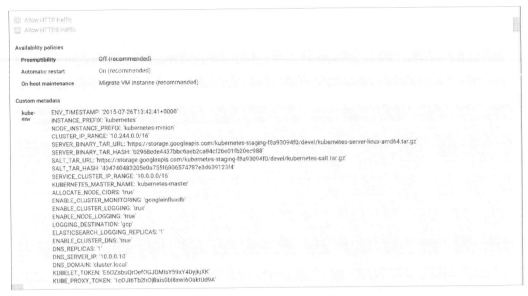

Figure 4.3. The GCE Instance template for minions

You'll see a number of settings, but the meat of the template is under **Custom** metadata. Here, you will see a number of environment variables and also a startup script that is run after a new machine instance is created. These are the core components that allow us to create new machines and have them automatically added to the available cluster nodes.

Because the template for new machines is already created, it is very simple to scale out our cluster in GCE. Simply go to the **Instance groups** located right above the **Instance templates** link on the side panel. Again, you should see a group titled **kubernetes-minion-group** or something similar. Click on that group to see the details, as shown in the following screenshot:

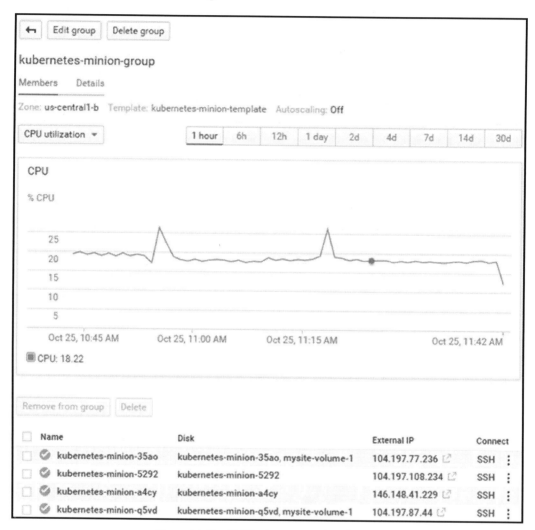

Figure 4.4. The GCE Instance group for minions

You'll see a page with a CPU metrics graph and four instances listed here. By default, the cluster creates four nodes. We can modify this group by clicking the **Edit group** button at the top of the page.

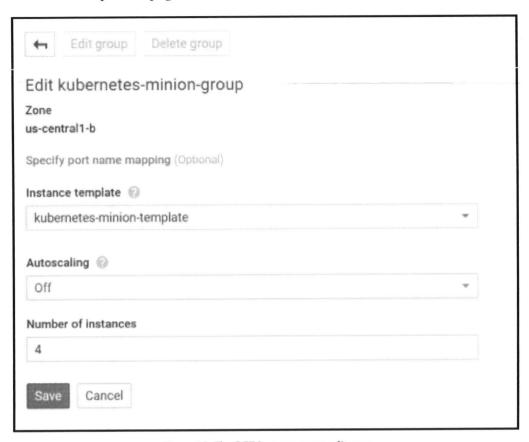

Figure 4.5. The GCE Instance group edit page

You should see **kubernetes-minion-template** selected in **Instance template** that we reviewed a moment ago. You'll also see an **Autoscaling** setting, which is **Off** by default and an instance count of 4. Simply, increment this to 5 and click on **Save**. You'll be taken back to the group details page and see a pop-up dialog showing the pending changes.

In a few minutes, you'll have a new instance listed on the details page. We can test that this is ready by using the get nodes command from the command line:

```
$ kubectl get nodes
```

# Autoscaling and scaling down

In the preceding example, we left autoscaling turned off. However, there may be some cases where you want to automatically scale your cluster up and down. Turning on autoscaling will allow you to choose a metric to monitor and scale on. A minimum and maximum number of instances can be defined as well as a cool down period between actions. For more information on autoscaling in GCE, refer to the link `https://cloud.google.com/compute/docs/autoscaler/?hl=en_US#scaling_based_on_cpu_utilization`.

**A word of caution on autoscaling and scale down in general**

First, if we repeat the earlier process and decrease the countdown to four, GCE will remove one node. However, it will not necessarily be the node you just added. The good news is that pods will be rescheduled on the remaining nodes. However, it can only reschedule where resources are available. If you are close to full capacity and shut down a node, there is a good chance that some pods will not have a place to be rescheduled. In addition, this is not a live migration, so any application state will be lost in the transition. The bottom line is that you should carefully consider the implications before scaling down or implementing an autoscaling scheme.

# Scaling up the cluster on AWS

The AWS provider code also makes it very easy to scale up your cluster. Similar to GCE, the AWS setup uses autoscaling groups to create the default four minion nodes.

This can also be easily modified using the CLI or the web console. In the console, from the EC2 page, simply go to the **Auto Scaling Groups** section at the bottom of the menu on the left. You should see a name similar to **kubernetes-minion-group**. Select that group and you will see details as shown in Figure 4.6:

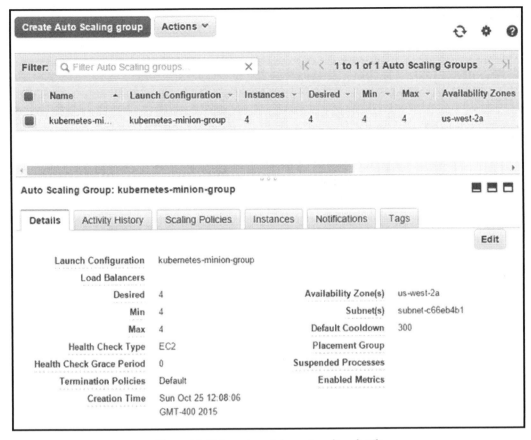

Figure 4.6. Kubernetes minion autoscaling details

We can scale this group up easily by clicking **Edit**. Then, change the **Desired**, **Min**, and **Max** values to 5 and click on **Save**. In a few minutes, you'll have the fifth node available. You can once again check this using the `get nodes` command.

Scaling down is the same process, but remember that we discussed the same considerations in the previous *Scaling the cluster on GCE* section. Workloads could get abandoned or at the very least unexpectedly restarted.

# Scaling manually

For other providers, creating new minions may not be an automated process. Depending on your provider, you'll need to perform various manual steps. It can be helpful to look at the provider-specific scripts under the `cluster` directory.

# Summary

We should now be a bit more comfortable with the basics of application scaling in Kubernetes. We also looked at the built-in functions in order to roll updates as well a manual process for testing and slowly integrating updates. Finally, we took a look at scaling the nodes of our underlying cluster and increasing overall capacity for our Kubernetes resources.

# 5
# Continuous Delivery

This chapter will show the reader how to integrate their build pipeline and deployments with a Kubernetes cluster. It will cover the concept of using Gulp.js and Jenkins in conjunction with your Kubernetes cluster.

This chapter will discuss the following topics:

- Integration with continuous deployment pipeline
- Using Gulp.js with Kubernetes
- Integrating Jenkins with Kubernetes

## Integration with continuous delivery

Continuous integration and delivery are key components to modern development shops. *Speed to market* or *mean-time-to-revenue* are crucial for any company that is creating their own software. We'll see how Kubernetes can help you.

CI/CD (short for **Continuous Integration/Continuous Delivery**) often requires ephemeral build and test servers to be available whenever changes are pushed to the code repository. Docker and Kubernetes are well suited for this task as it's easy to create containers in a few seconds and just as easy to remove them after builds are run. In addition, if you already have a large portion of infrastructure available on your cluster, it can make sense to utilize the idle capacity for builds and testing.

In this chapter, we will explore two popular tools used in building and deploying software. Gulp.js is a simple task runner used to automate the build process using **JavaScript** and **Node.js**. **Jenkins** is a fully-fledged continuous integration server.

# Gulp.js

**Gulp.js** gives us the framework to do *Build as code*. Similar to *Infrastructure as code*, this allows us to programmatically define our build process. We will walk through a short example to demonstrate how you can create a complete workflow from a Docker image build to the final Kubernetes Service.

# Prerequisites

For this section, you will need a **NodeJS** environment installed and ready including the **node package manage (npm)**. If you do not already have these packages installed, you can find instructions at `https://docs.npmjs.com/getting-started/installing-node`.

You can check whether NodeJS is installed correctly with a `node -v` command.

You'll also need the **Docker CLI** and a **DockerHub** account to push a new image. You can find instructions to install the Docker CLI at `https://docs.docker.com/installation/`.

You can easily create a DockerHub account at `https://hub.docker.com/`.

After you have your credentials, you can log in with the CLI using `$ docker login`.

# Gulp build example

Let's start by creating a project directory named `node-gulp`:

```
$ mkdir node-gulp
$ cd node-gulp
```

Next, we will install the `gulp` package and check whether it's ready by running the `npm` command with the version flag as follows:

```
$ npm install -g gulp
```

You may need to open a new terminal window to make sure that `gulp` is on your path. Also, make sure to navigate back to your `node-gulp` directory:

```
$ gulp -v
```

Next, we will install gulp locally in our project folder as well as the `gulp-git` and `gulp-shell` plugins as follows:

```
$ npm install --save-dev gulp
$ npm install gulp-git -save
$ npm install --save-dev gulp-shell
```

Finally, we need to create a Kubernetes controller and service definition file as well as a `gulpfile.js` to run all our tasks. Again, these files are available in the book file bundle if you wish to copy them instead. Refer to the following code:

```yaml
apiVersion: v1
kind: ReplicationController
metadata:
  name: node-gulp
  labels:
    name: node-gulp
spec:
  replicas: 1
  selector:
    name: node-gulp
  template:
    metadata:
      labels:
        name: node-gulp
    spec:
      containers:
      - name: node-gulp
        image: <your username>/node-gulp:latest
        imagePullPolicy: Always
        ports:
        - containerPort: 80
```

*Listing 5-1*: `node-gulp-controller.yaml`

As you can see, we have a basic controller. You will need to replace **<your username>**/node-gulp:latest with your username:

```yaml
apiVersion: v1
kind: Service
metadata:
  name: node-gulp
  labels:
    name: node-gulp
spec:
  type: LoadBalancer
  ports:
  - name: http
    protocol: TCP
    port: 80
  selector:
    name: node-gulp
```

*Listing 5-2*: `node-gulp-service.yaml`

Next, we have a simple service that selects the pods from our controller and creates an external load balancer for access as follows:

```javascript
var gulp = require('gulp');
var git = require('gulp-git');
var shell = require('gulp-shell');

// Clone a remote repo
gulp.task('clone', function(){
  return git.clone('https://github.com/jonbaierCTP/getting-
    started-with-kubernetes.git', function (err) {
    if (err) throw err;
  });

});


// Update codebase
gulp.task('pull', function(){
  return git.pull('origin', 'master', {cwd: './getting-started-
    with-kubernetes'}, function (err) {
    if (err) throw err;
  });
});


//Build Docker Image
gulp.task('docker-build', shell.task([
  'docker build -t <your username>/node-gulp ./getting-started-
    with-kubernetes/ docker-image-source/container-info/',
  'docker push <your username>/node-gulp'
]));


//Run New Pod
gulp.task('create-kube-pod', shell.task([
  'kubectl create -f node-gulp-controller.yaml',
  'kubectl create -f node-gulp-service.yaml'
]));


//Update Pod
gulp.task('update-kube-pod', shell.task([
  'kubectl delete -f node-gulp-controller.yaml',
  'kubectl create -f node-gulp-controller.yaml'
]));
```

*Listing 5-3:* `gulpfile.js`

Finally, we have the `gulpfile.js` file. This is where all our build tasks are defined. Again, fill in your username in both the **<your username>**/node-gulp sections.

Looking through the file, first, the clone task downloads our image source code from GitHub. The pull tasks execute a `git` pull on the cloned repository. Next, the `docker-build` command builds an image from the `container-info` subfolder and pushes it to DockerHub. Finally, we have the `create-kube-pod` and `update-kube-pod` command. As you can guess, the `create-kube-pod` command creates our controller and service for the first time, whereas the `update-kube-pod` command simply replaces the controller.

Let's go ahead and run these commands and see our end-to-end workflow.

```
$ gulp clone
$ gulp docker-build
```

The first time through you can run the `create-kube-pod` command as follows:

```
$ gulp create-kube-pod
```

This is all there is to it. If we run a quick `kubectl` describe command for the node-gulp service, we can get the external IP for our new service. Browse to that IP and you'll see the familiar `container-info` application running. Note that the host starts with `node-gulp`, just as we named it in the previously mentioned pod definition.

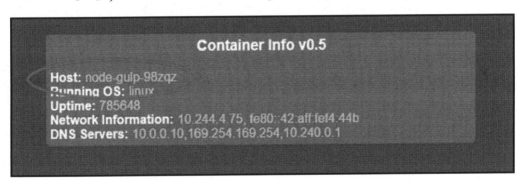

Figure 5.1. Service launched by Gulp build

On subsequent updates, run `pull` and `update-kube-pod`, as shown here:

```
$ gulp pull
$ gulp docker-build
$ gulp update-kube-pod
```

This is a very simple example, but you can begin to see how easy it is to coordinate your build and deployment end to end with a few simple lines of code. Next, we will look at using Kubernetes to actually run builds using Jenkins.

# Kubernetes plugin for Jenkins

One way we can use Kubernetes for our CI/CD pipeline is to run our Jenkins build slaves in a containerized environment. Luckily, there is already a plugin, written by Carlos Sanchez, which allows you to run Jenkins slaves in Kubernetes' pods.

## Prerequisites

You'll need a Jenkins server handy for this next example. If you don't have one you can use, there is a Docker image available at `https://hub.docker.com/_/jenkins/`.

Running it from the Docker CLI is as simple as this:

```
docker run --name myjenkins -p 8080:8080 -v /var/jenkins_home jenkins
```

## Installing plugins

Log in to your Jenkins server, and from your home dashboard, click on **Manage Jenkins**. Then, select **Manage Plugins** from the list.

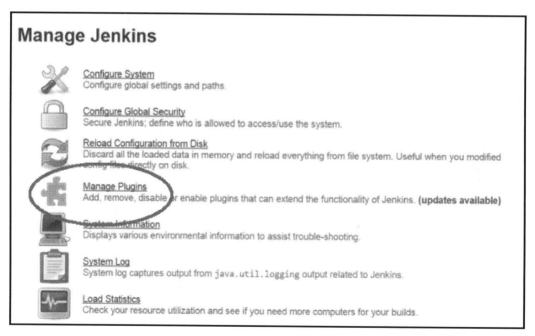

Figure 5.2. Jenkins main dashboard

The credentials plugin is required, but should be installed by default. We can check the **Installed** tab if in doubt, as shown in the following screenshot:

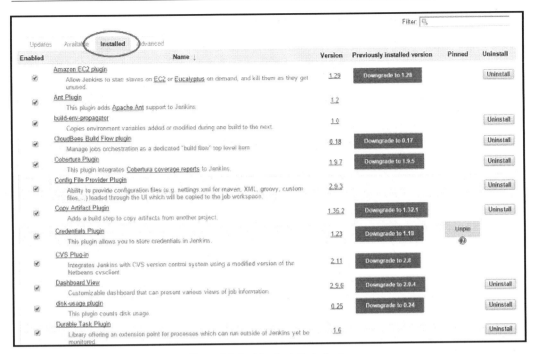

Figure 5.3. Jenkins installed plugins

Next, we can click on the **Available** tab. The Kubernetes plugin should be located under **Cluster Management and Distributed Build** or **Misc (cloud)**. There are many plugins, so you can alternatively search for Kubernetes on the page. Check the box for **Kubernetes Plugin** and click on **Install without restart**.

This will install the **Kubernetes Plugin** and the **Durable Task Plugin**.

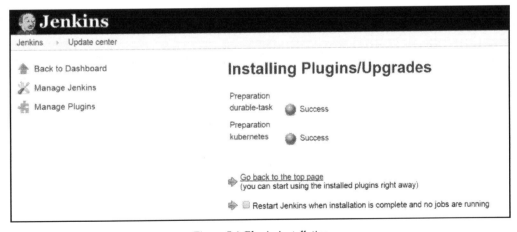

Figure 5.4. Plugin installation

If you wish to install a nonstandard version or just like to tinker, you can optionally download the plugins. The latest **Kubernetes** and **Durable Task** plugins can be found here:

- Kubernetes plugin: `https://wiki.jenkins-ci.org/display/JENKINS/Kubernetes+Plugin`
- Durable Task plugin: `https://wiki.jenkins-ci.org/display/JENKINS/Durable+Task+Plugin`

Next, we can click on the **Advanced** tab and scroll down to **Upload Plugin**. Navigate to the `durable-task.hpi` file and click on **Upload**. You should see a screen that shows an installing progress bar. After a minute or two, it will update to **Success**.

Finally, install the main Kubernetes plugin. On the left-hand side, click on **Manage Plugins** and then the **Advanced** tab once again. This time, upload the `kubernetes.hpi` file and click on **Upload**. After a few minutes, the installation should be complete.

# Configuring the Kubernetes plugin

Click on **Back to Dashboard** or the **Jenkins** link in the top-left corner. From the main dashboard page, click on the **Credentials** link. Choose a domain from the list; in my case, I just used the default **Global** credentials domain. Click on **Add Credentials**.

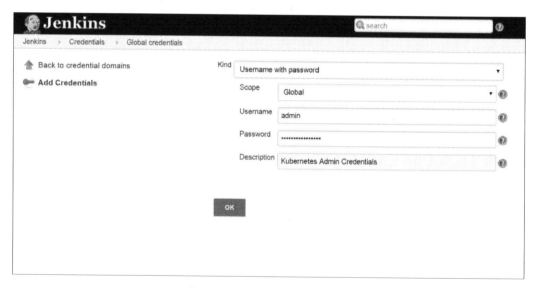

Figure 5.5. Add credentials screen

Leave **Kind** as **Username with password** and **Scope** as **Global**. Add your Kubernetes admin credentials. Remember that you can find these by running the `config` command:

```
$ kubectl config view
```

Give it a sensible description and click on **OK**.

Now that we have our credentials saved, we can add our Kubernetes server. Click on the **Jenkins** link in the top-left corner and then **Manage Jenkins**. From there, select **Configure System** and scroll all the way down to the **Cloud** section. Select **Kubernetes** from the **Add a new cloud** dropdown and a **Kubernetes** section will appear as follows:

Figure 5.6. New Kubernetes cloud settings

You'll need to specify the URL for your master in the form of `https://<Master IP>/`.

Next, choose the credentials we added from the drop-down list. Since Kubernetes use a self-signed certificate by default, you'll also need to check the **Disable https certificate check** checkbox.

Click **Test Connection** and if all goes well, you should see **Connection successful** appearing next to the button.

> If you are using an older version of the plugin, you may not see the **Disable https certificate check** checkbox. If this is the case, you will need to install the self-signed certificate directly on the **Jenkins Master**.

Finally, we will add a pod template by choosing **Kubernetes Pod Template** from the **Add Pod Template** dropdown next to **Images**.

This will create another new section. Use `jenkins-slave` for the **Name** and **Labels** section. Use `csanchez/jenkins-slave` for the **Docker Image** and leave `/home/ jenkins` for the **Jenkins Slave** root directory.

> Labels can be used later on in the build settings to force the build to use the Kubernetes cluster.

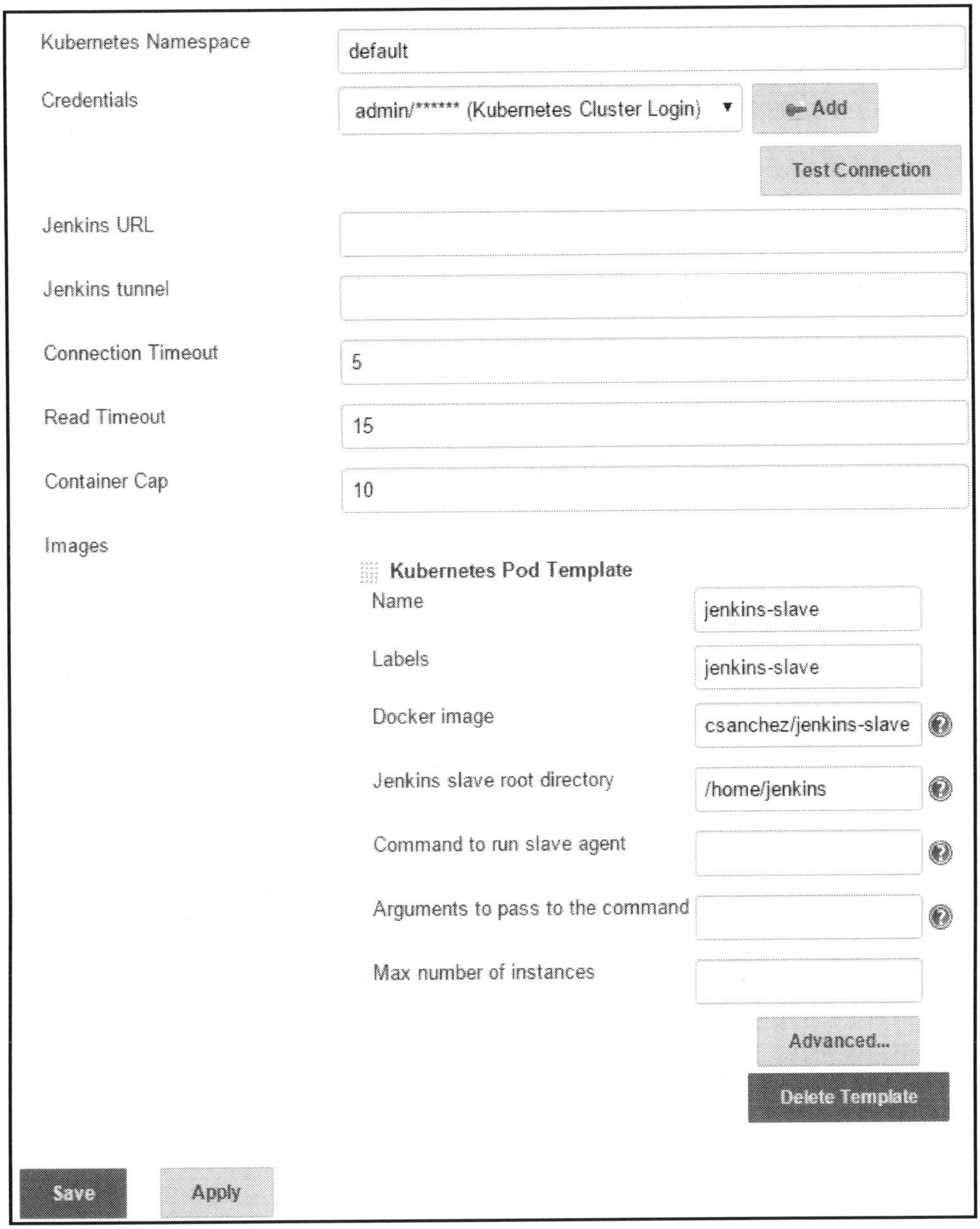

| Kubernetes Namespace | default |
| --- | --- |
| Credentials | admin/****** (Kubernetes Cluster Login) ▼   🔑 Add |
| | Test Connection |
| Jenkins URL | |
| Jenkins tunnel | |
| Connection Timeout | 5 |
| Read Timeout | 15 |
| Container Cap | 10 |
| Images | |

⠿ **Kubernetes Pod Template**

| Name | jenkins-slave |
| --- | --- |
| Labels | jenkins-slave |
| Docker image | csanchez/jenkins-slave ⓘ |
| Jenkins slave root directory | /home/jenkins ⓘ |
| Command to run slave agent | ⓘ |
| Arguments to pass to the command | ⓘ |
| Max number of instances | |

Advanced...

Delete Template

Save   Apply

Figure 5.7. Kubernetes pod template

Click on **Save** and you are all set. Now builds can use the slaves in the Kubernetes pod we just created.

There is another note about firewalls. The Jenkins Master will need to be reachable by the all machines in your Kubernetes cluster as the pod could land anywhere. You can find out your port settings in Jenkins under **Manage Jenkins** and **Configure Global Security**.

# Bonus fun

**Fabric8** bills itself as an integration platform. It includes a variety of logging, monitoring, and continuous delivery tools. It also has a nice console, an API registry, and a 3D game that lets you shoot at your pods. It's a very cool project, and it actually runs on Kubernetes. Refer to `http://fabric8.io/`.

It's an easy single command to set up on your Kubernetes cluster, so refer to `http://fabric8.io/guide/getStarted/gke.html`.

# Summary

We looked at two continuous integration tools that can be used with Kubernetes. We did a brief walk-through of deploying Gulp.js task on our cluster. We also looked at a new plugin to integrate Jenkins build slaves into your Kubernetes cluster. You should now have a better sense of how Kubernetes can integrate with your own CI/CD pipeline.

# 6
# Monitoring and Logging

This chapter will cover the usage and customization of both built-in and third-party monitoring tools on our Kubernetes cluster. We will cover how to use the tools to monitor health and performance of our cluster. In addition, we will look at built-in logging, the **Google Cloud Logging** service, and **Sysdig**.

This chapter will discuss the following topics:

- How Kuberentes uses cAdvisor, Heapster, InfluxDB, and Grafana
- How to customize the default Grafana dashboard
- How FluentD and Grafana are used
- How to install and use logging tools
- How to work with popular third-party tools, such as StackDriver and Sysdig, to extend our monitoring capabilities

## Monitoring operations

Real-world monitoring goes far beyond checking whether a system is up and running. Although health checks, like those you learned in *Chapter 2, Kubernetes – Core Concepts and Constructs*, under the *Health checks* section, can help us isolate problem applications. Operation teams can best serve the business when they can anticipate the issues and mitigate them before a system goes offline.

Best practices in monitoring are to measure the performance and usage of core resources and watch for trends that stray from the normal baseline. Containers are not different here, and a key component to managing our Kubernetes cluster is having a clear view into performance and availability of the OS, network, system (CPU and memory), and storage resources across all nodes.

In this chapter, we will examine several options to monitor and measure the performance and availability of all our cluster resources. In addition, we will look at a few options for alerting and notifications when irregular trends start to emerge.

# Built-in monitoring

If you recall from *Chapter 1, Kubernetes and Container Operations*, we noted that our nodes were already running a number of monitoring services. We can see these once again by running the `get pods` command with the `kube-system` namespace specified as follows:

```
$ kubectl get pods --namespace=kube-system
```

The following screenshot is the result of the preceding command:

```
NAME                                               READY   STATUS    RESTARTS   AGE
fluentd-cloud-logging-kubernetes-minion-lxhu       1/1     Running   0          1d
fluentd-cloud-logging-kubernetes-minion-merd       1/1     Running   0          1d
fluentd-cloud-logging-kubernetes-minion-pjl5       1/1     Running   0          1d
fluentd-cloud-logging-kubernetes-minion-vgjn       1/1     Running   0          1d
kube-dns-v8-8qtzl                                  4/4     Running   1          1d
kube-ui-v1-x4wuf                                   1/1     Running   0          1d
monitoring-heapster-v6-f1eqm                       1/1     Running   1          1d
monitoring-influx-grafana-v1-eikyn                 2/2     Running   0          1d
```

Figure 6.1. System pod listing

Again, we see a variety of services, but how does this all fit together? If you recall the *Node (formerly minions)* section from *Chapter 2, Kubernetes – Core Concepts and Constructs*, each node is running a kublet. The kublet is the main interface for nodes to interact and update the API server. One such update is the **metrics** of the node resources. The actual reporting of the resource usage is performed by a program named cAdvisor.

**cAdvisor** is another open source project from Google, which provides various metrics on container resource use. Metrics include CPU, memory, and network statistics. There is no need to tell cAdvisor about individual containers; it collects the metrics for all containers on a node and reports this back to the kublet, which in turn reports to Heapster.

**Google's open source projects**

Google has a variety of open source projects related to Kubernetes. Check them out, use them, and even contribute your own code!

cAdvisor and Heapster are mentioned in the following section:

- **cAdvisor**: `https://github.com/google/cadvisor`
- **Heapster**: `https://github.com/kubernetes/heapster`

**Contrib** is a catch-all for a variety of components that are not part of core Kubernetes. It is found at `https://github.com/kubernetes/contrib`.

**LevelDB** is a key store library that was used in the creation of InfluxDB. It is found at `https://github.com/google/leveldb`.

**Heapster** is yet another open source project from Google; you may start to see a theme emerging here (see the preceding information box). Heapster runs in a container on one of the minion nodes and aggregates the data from kublet. A simple REST interface is provided to query the data.

When using the GCE setup, a few additional packages are set up for us, which saves us time and gives us a complete package to monitor our container workloads. As we can see from Figure 6.1, there is another pod with `influx-grafana` in the title.

**InfluxDB** is described at it's official website as follows[1]:

*An open-source distributed time series database with no external dependencies.*

It is based on a key store package (see the previous *Google's open source projects* information box) and is perfect to store and query event or time-based statistics such as those provided by Heapster.

Finally, we have **Grafana**, which provides a dashboard and graphing interface for the data stored in InfluxDB. Using Grafana, users can create a custom monitoring dashboard and get immediate visibility into the health of their Kubernetes cluster and therefore their entire container infrastructure.

# Exploring Heapster

Let's quickly look at the REST interface by SSH'ing to the node with the Heapster pod. First, we can list the pods to find the one running Heapster as follows:

```
$ kubectl get pods --namespace=kube-system
```

The name of the pod should start with `monitoring-heapster`. Run a `describe` command to see which node it is running on as follows:

```
$ kubectl describe pods/<Heapster monitoring Pod> --namespace=kube-system
```

From the output in the following figure (Figure 6.2), we can see that the pod is running in `kubernetes-minion-merd`. Also note the IP for the pod, a few lines down, as we will need that in a moment.

```
Name:                        monitoring-heapster-v6-f1eqm
Namespace:                   kube-system
Image(s):                    gcr.io/google_containers/heapster:v0.16.1
Node:                        kubernetes-minion-merd/10.240.171.87
Labels:                      k8s-app=heapster,kubernetes.io/cluster-service=tr
ue,version=v6
Status:                      Running
Reason:
Message:
IP:                          10.244.2.3
Replication Controllers:     monitoring-heapster-v6 (1/1 replicas created)
Containers:
  heapster:
    Image:        gcr.io/google_containers/heapster:v0.16.1
    Limits:
      cpu:                   100m
      memory:                300Mi
    State:                   Running
      Started:               Sat, 19 Sep 2015 10:36:36 -0400
    Ready:                   True
    Restart Count:           1
Conditions:
  Type           Status
  Ready          True
No events.
```

Figure 6.2. Heapster pod details

Next, we can SSH to this box with the familiar `gcloud ssh` command as follows:

```
$ gcloud compute --project "<Your project ID>" ssh --zone "<your gce zone>" "<kubernetes minion from describe>"
```

From here, we can access the `Heapster` REST API directly using the pod's IP address. Remember that pod IPs are routable not only in the containers but also on the nodes themselves. The `Heapster` API is listening on port `8082`, and we can get a full list of metrics at `/api/v1/metric-export-schema/`.

Let's see the list now by issuing a `curl` command to the pod IP address we saved from the `describe` command as follows:

```
$ curl -G <Heapster IP from describe>:8082/api/v1/metric-export-schema/
```

We will see a listing that is quite long. The first section shows all the metrics available. The last two sections list fields by which we can filter and group. For your convenience, I've added the following tables that are a little bit easier to read:

| Metric | Description | Unit | Type |
|---|---|---|---|
| uptime | The number of milliseconds since the container was started | ms | cumulative |
| cpu/usage | Cumulative CPU usage on all cores | ns | cumulative |
| cpu/limit | CPU limit in millicores | - | gauge |
| memory/usage | Total memory usage | bytes | gauge |
| memory/working_set | Total working set usage. Working set is the memory being used and not easily dropped by the kernel | bytes | gauge |
| memory/limit | Memory limit | bytes | gauge |
| memory/page_faults | The number of page faults | - | cumulative |
| memory/major_page_faults | The number of major page faults | - | cumulative |
| network/rx | Cumulative number of bytes received over the network | bytes | cumulative |
| network/rx_errors | Cumulative number of errors while receiving over the network | - | cumulative |
| network/tx | Cumulative number of bytes sent over the network | bytes | cumulative |
| network/tx_errors | Cumulative number of errors while sending over the network | - | cumulative |
| filesystem/usage | Total number of bytes consumed on a filesystem | bytes | gauge |
| filesystem/limit | The total size of filesystem in bytes | bytes | gauge |

Table 6.1. Available Heapster metrics

| Field | Description | Label type |
|---|---|---|
| hostname | The hostname where the container ran | Common |
| host_id | An identifier specific to a host, which is set by cloud provider or user | Common |
| container_name | The user-provided name of the container or full container name for system containers | Common |
| pod_name | The name of the pod | Pod |
| pod_id | The unique ID of the pod | Pod |
| pod_namespace | The namespace of the pod | Pod |
| namespace_id | The unique ID of the namespace of the pod | Pod |
| labels | A comma-separated list of user-provided labels | Pod |

Table 6.2. Available Heapster fields

# Customizing our dashboards

Now that we have the fields, we can have some fun. Recall the Grafana page we looked at in *Chapter 1, Kubernetes and Container Operations*. Let's pull that up again by going our cluster's monitoring URL. Note that you may need to log in with your cluster credentials. Refer to the following format of the link you need to use:

```
https://<your master IP>/api/v1/proxy/namespaces/kube-system/
services/monitoring-grafana
```

We'll see the default Kubernetes dashboard, and now we can add our own statistics to the board. Scroll all the way to the bottom and click on **Add a Row**. This should create a space for a new row and present a green tab on the left-hand side of the screen.

Let's start by adding a view into the filesystem usage for each node (minion). Click on the *green* tab to expand and then choose **Add Panel** and then **graph**. An empty graph should appear on the screen. If we click on the **graph** where it says **no title (click here)**, a context menu will appear. We can then click on **Edit**, and we'll be able to set up the query for our custom dashboard panel.

The **series** box allows us to use any of the Heapster metrics we saw in the previous tables. In the **series** box, enter filesystem/usage_bytes_gauge and select to **max(value)**. Then, enter 5s for **group by time** and **hostname** in the box marked column next to the plus sign, as shown in the following screenshot:

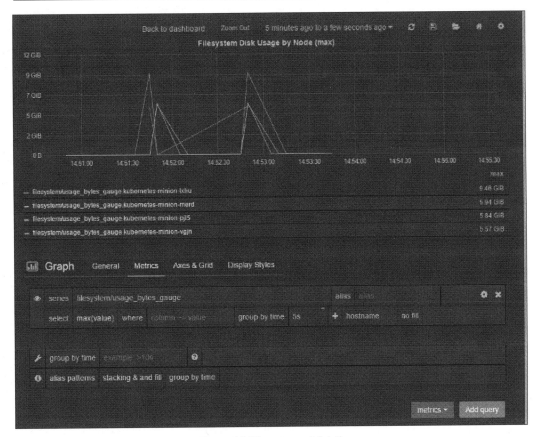

Figure 6.3. Heapster pod details

Next, let's click on the **Axes & Grid** tab, so that we can set the units and legend. Under **Left Y Axis**, set **Format** to **bytes** and **Label** to **Disk Space Used**. Under **Right Y Axis**, set **Format** to **none**. Next, under **Legend** styles, make sure to check **Show values, and table**. A **Legend Values** section should appear, and we can check the box for **Max** here.

Now, let's quickly go to the **General** tab and choose a title. In my case, I named mine `Filesystem Disk Usage by Node (max)`.

We don't want to lose this nice new graph we've created, so let's click on the save icon in the top right corner. It looks like a *floppy disk* (you can do a Google image search if you don't know what those are).

After we click on the save icon, a dropdown will appear with several options. The first item should have the default dashboard title, which is **Kubernetes Cluster!** at the time of this writing. Also, click on the save icon on the right-hand side.

It should take us back to the main dashboard where we will see our new graph at the bottom. Let's add another panel to that row. Again use the *green* tab and then select **Add Panel** and **singlestat**. Once again, an empty panel will appear, and we can click it where it says **no title (click here)** for the context menu and then click on **Edit**.

Let's say, we want to watch a particular node and monitor memory usage. We can easily do this by setting the where clause in our query. First, choose **network/rx_bytes_cumulative** for **series** and **mean(value)** for **select**. Then, we can specify the hostname in the `where` clause with `hostname=kubernetes-minion-35ao` and **group by time** to 5s. (Use one of your own hostnames if you are following along).

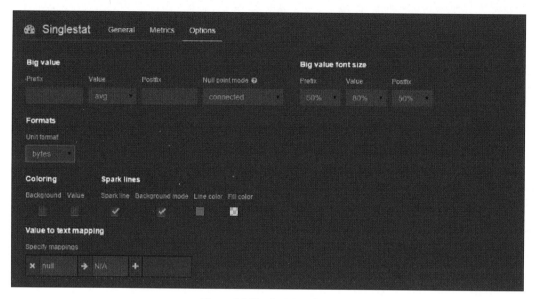

Figure 6.4. Singlestat options

Under the **Options** tab, make sure that **Unit format** is set to **bytes** and check the **Spark line** box under **Spark lines**. The **sparkline** gives us a quick history view of the recent variation in the value. We can use the **Background** mode to take up the entire background; by default, it uses the area below the value.

> Under **Coloring**, we can optionally check the **Value** box. A **Thresholds** and **Colors** section will appear. This will allow us to choose different colors for the value based on the threshold tier we specify. Note that an unformatted version of the number must be used for threshold values.

Now, let's go back to the **General** tab and choose a title as **Network bytes received (Node 35ao)**. Once again, let's save our work and return to the dashboard. We should now have a row that looks like the following figure (Figure 6.5):

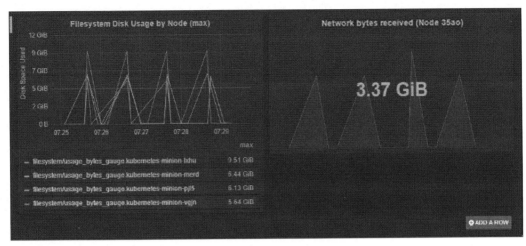

Figure 6.5. Custom dashboard panels

A third type of panel we didn't cover is **text**. It's pretty straightforward and allows us to place a block of text on the dashboard using HTML, markdown, or just plain text.

As we can see, it is pretty easy to build a custom dashboard and monitor the health of our cluster at a glance.

# FluentD and Google Cloud Logging

Looking back at Figure 6.1, you may have noted a number of pods starting with the words **fluentd-cloud-logging-kubernetes**. These pods appear when using the GCE provider for your K8s cluster. A pod like this exists on every node in our cluster and its sole purpose to handle the processing of Kubernetes logs.

If we log in to our Google Cloud Platform account, we can see some of the logs processed there. Simply navigate to our project page, and on the left, under **Monitoring**, click on **Logs**. (If you are using the beta console, it will be under **Operations** and then **Logging**.) This will take us to a log listing page with a number of drop-down menus on the top. If this is your first time visiting the page, you should see a log selection dropdown with the value **All Logs**.

In this dropdown, we'll see a number of Kubernetes-related entries, including **kublet** and some entries with **kubernetes** at the beginning of the label. We can also filter by date and use the *play* button to watch events stream in live.

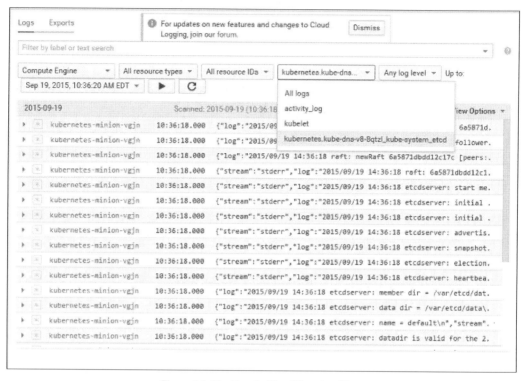

Figure 6.6. The Google Cloud Logging filter

# FluentD

Now we know that the `fluentd-cloud-logging-kubernetes` pods are sending the data to the Google Cloud, but why do we need FluentD? Simply put, **FluentD** is a collector. It can be configured to have multiple sources to collect and tag logs, which are then sent to various output points for analysis, alerting, or archiving. We can even transform data using plugins before it is passed on to its destination.

Not all provider setups have FluentD installed by default, but it is one of the recommended approaches to give us greater flexibility for future monitoring operations. The AWS Kubernetes setup also uses FluentD, but instead forwards events to **Elasticsearch**.

**Exploring FluentD**

If you are curious about the inner workings of the FluentD setup or just want to customize the log collection, we can explore quite easily using the `kubectl exec` command.

First, let's see if we can find the FluentD `config` file:

```
$ kubectl exec fluentd-cloud-logging-kubernetes-minion-
35ao --namespace=kube-system -- ls /etc
```

Usually, we would look in the `etc` folder for a `ta-agent` or `fluent` subfolder. However, if we run an `ls` command, we'll see that there is no `ta-agent` or `fluent` subfolder, but there is a `google-fluentd` subfolder:

```
$ kubectl exec fluentd-cloud-logging-kubernetes-minion-
35ao --namespace=kube-system -- ls /etc/google-fluentd/
```

While searching in this directory, we should see a `google-fluentd.conf` file. We can view that file with a simple `cat` command as follows:

```
$ kubectl exec fluentd-cloud-logging-kubernetes-minion-
35ao --namespace=kube-system -- cat /etc/google-fluentd/
google-fluentd.conf
```

We should see a number of sources including the `kublet`, `containers`, `etcd`, and various other Kubernetes components.

Note that while we can make changes here, remember that is a running container and our changes won't be saved if the pod dies or is restarted. If we really want to customize, it's best to use this container as a base and build a new container that we can push to a repository for later use.

# Maturing our monitoring operations

While Grafana gives us a great start to monitor our container operations, it is still a work in progress. In the real world of operations, having a complete dashboard view is great once we know there is a problem. However, in everyday scenarios, we'd prefer to be proactive and actually receive notifications when issues arise. This kind of alerting capability is a must to keep the operations team ahead of the curve and out of *reactive mode*.

There are many solutions available in this space, and we will take a look at two in particular: GCE monitoring (StackDriver) and Sysdig.

# GCE (StackDriver)

**StackDriver** is a great place to start for infrastructure in the public cloud. It is actually owned by Google, so it's integrated as the Google Cloud Platform monitoring service. Before your lock-in alarm bells start ringing, StackDriver also has solid integration with AWS. In addition, StackDriver has alerting capability with support for notification to a variety of platforms and webhooks for anything else.

## Sign-up for GCE monitoring

In the GCE console, under the **Monitoring** section, there is a **Dashboard & alerts** link (or just the **Monitoring** link under **Operations** in the beta console). This will open a new window where we can enable the monitoring functionality (still in beta at the time of this writing). Once enabled, we'll be taken to a screen that has install instructions for each operating system (this will be under **Set up and monitor an endpoint** in the beta console). It will also show your API key, which is necessary for the installation.

If you want to do something similar in AWS, you can simply sign up for account at StackDriver's main website:

`https://www.stackdriver.com/`

Installation instructions for the more common installs can be found at `http://support.stackdriver.com/customer/en/portal/articles/1491726-what-is-the-stackdriver-agent`.

We can find our API key under **Account Settings** and **API Keys**.

Click on **Go to Monitoring** to proceed. We'll be taken to the main dashboard page where we will see some basic statistics on our node in the cluster. If we go to **Infrastructure** and then **Instances**, we'll be taken to a page with all our nodes listed. By clicking on the individual node, we can again see some basic information even without an agent installed.

# Configure detailed monitoring

As we have seen, simply enabling monitoring will give us basic stats for all our machines in GCE, but if we want to get detailed results, we'll need the agent on each node. Let's walk through an install.

As before, we'll want to use the `gcloud compute ssh` command to get a shell on one of our minion nodes. Then, we can download and install the agent. If you need your API key, this can be found by clicking your user icon in the top-right corner and going to **Account Settings** and then on the next page, click on **API Keys** in the menu on the left:

```
$ curl -O https://repo.stackdriver.com/stack-install.sh
$ sudo bash stack-install.sh --api-key=<API-KEY>
```

If everything goes well, we should have an agent installed and ready. We can check this by running the `info` command as follows:

```
$ /opt/stackdriver/stack-config info
```

We should see a lot of information in the form of JSON on the screen. After you finish, give the agent a few minutes before going back to **Infrastructure** and **Instances**.

On the summary instance page, we'll note that all our GCE instances are showing CPU usage. However, only the instance with the agent installed will show the **Memory usage** statistic.

Click on the node with the agent installed, so we can inspect it a bit further. If we click on each one and look at the details page, we should note that the instance with the agent installed has a lot more information. Although all instances report CPU usage, Disk I/O, and network traffic, the instance with the agent has much more.

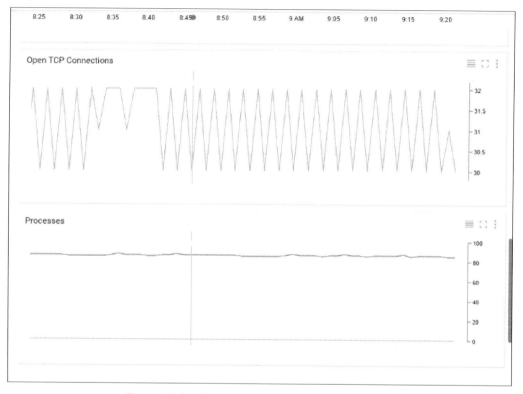

Figure 6.7. Google Cloud Monitoring with agent installed

In Figure 6.7, we can see a variety of additional charts including Open TCP connections and processes as well as CPU steal (not pictured). We also have better visibility into the machine details such as network interfaces, file systems, and operating system information.

Now that we see how much information is available, we can install the agent on the remaining instances. You may also wish to install an agent on the master as it is a critical piece of your Kubernetes infrastructure.

# Alerts

Next, we can look at the alerting policies available as part of the monitoring service. From the instance details page, click on the **Create Alerting Policy** button in the **Incidents** section at the top of the page.

We'll name the policy as `Excessive CPU Load` and set a metric threshold. Under the section, in the **Metric Threshold** area, click on **Next** and then in the **TARGET** section, set **Resource Type** to **Instances**. Then, set **Applies To** to **Group** and **kubernetes**. Leave **Condition Triggers If** set to **Any Member Violates**.

Click on **Next** and leave **IF METRIC** as **CPU (agent)** and **CONDITION** as **above**. Now set **THRESHOLD (PERCENT)** to `80` and leave the time under **FOR** to **5 minutes**. Click on **Save Condition**.

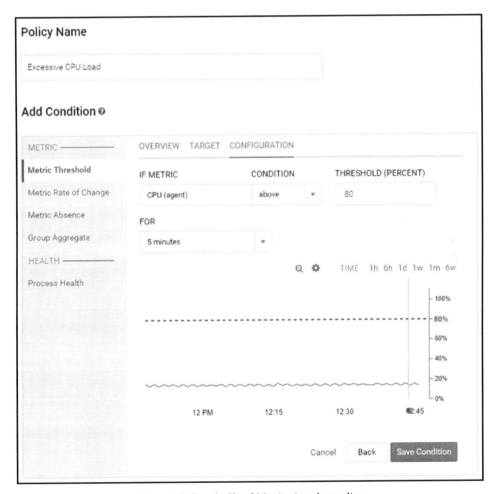

Figure 6.8. Google Cloud Monitoring alert policy

Finally, we will add a notification. Under that section, leave **Method** as **Email** and click on **Add Notification**. Enter your e-mail address and then click on **Save Policy**.

Now whenever the CPU from one of our instances goes above 80 percent, we will receive an e-mail notification. If we ever need to review our policies, we can find them under the **Alerting** dropdown and **Policies Overview** at the menu on the top of the screen.

# Beyond system monitoring with Sysdig

Monitoring our cloud systems is a great start, but what about visibility into the containers themselves? Although there are a variety of cloud monitoring and visibility tools, Sysdig stands out for its ability to dive deep not only into system operations but specifically containers.

Sysdig is open source and is billed as *a universal system visibility tool with native support for containers*[2]. It is a command-line tool, which provides insight into the areas we've looked at earlier such as storage, network, and system processes. What sets it apart is the level of detail and visibility it offers for these process and system activities. Furthermore, it has native support for containers, which gives us a full picture of our container operations. This is a highly recommended tool for your container operations arsenal. Their main website is `http://www.sysdig.org/`.

## Sysdig Cloud

We will take a look at the Sysdig tool and some of the useful command-line-based UIs in a moment. However, the team at Sysdig has also built a commercial product, named **Sysdig Cloud**, which provides the advanced dashboard, alerting, and notification services we discussed earlier in the chapter. Also, the differentiator here has high visibility into containers, including some nice visualizations of our application topology.

 If you'd rather skip the *Sysdig Cloud* section and just try out the command-line tool, simply skip to the *Sysdig command line* section later in this chapter.

If you have not done so already, sign up for Sysdig Cloud at `http://www.sysdigcloud.com`.

After activating and logging in for the first time, we'll be taken to a welcome page. Clicking on **Next**, we are shown a page with various options to install the `sysdig` agents. For our example environment, we will use a Linux agent. The **Next** button will be disabled until we install at least one agent. The page should show the following command with our *access key* filled in.

```
curl -s https://s3.amazonaws.com/download.draios.com/stable/install-agent
| sudo bash -s -- --access_key <Your Access Key>
```

We'll need to SSH into our master and each node to run the installer. It will take a few minutes to install several packages and then set up the connection to the Sysdig Cloud.

After our first install completes, the page should update with the text **You have one agent connected!** and the **Next** button will become active. Go ahead and install the rest of the agents and then come back to this page and click on **Next**.

We can skip the AWS setup for now and then click on **Let's Get Started** on the final screen.

We'll be taken to the main **sysdig cloud** dashboard screen. **kubernetes-master** and our various minion nodes should appear under the **Explore** tab. We should see something similar to Figure 6.9 with our cluster master and all four minion nodes (or the nodes we have already installed agents on).

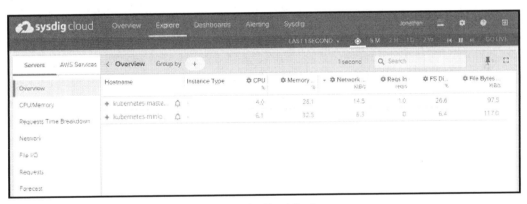

Figure 6.9. Sysdig Cloud Explore page

This page shows us a table view and the links on the left let us explore some key metrics for CPU, memory, networking, and so on. Although this is a great start, the detailed views will give us a much deeper look at each node.

# Detailed views

Let's take a look at these views. Select **kubernetes-master** and then scroll down to the detail section that appears below. By default, we should see the **System: Overview by Process** view (If it's not selected, just click on it in the list on the left.) If the chart is hard to read, simply use the maximize icon in the top-left corner of each graph for a larger view.

There are a variety of interesting views to explore. Just to call out a few others, **Application: HTTP** and **System: Overview** by container give us some great charts for inspection. In the later view, we can see stats for CPU, memory, network, and file usage by container.

# Topology views

In addition, there are three topology views at the bottom. These views are perfect for helping us understand how our application is communicating. Click on **Topology: Network Traffic** and wait a few seconds for the view to fully populate. It should look similar to Figure 6.10:

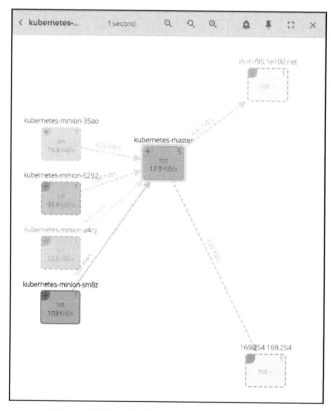

Figure 6.10. Sysdig Cloud network topology view

We note the view maps out the flow of communication between the minion nodes and the master in the cluster. On the right-hand side, there may be connections to servers with a **1e100.net** name and also **169.254.169.254**, which are both part of Google infrastructure.

You may also note a **+** symbol in the top corner of the node boxes. Click on that in **kubernetes-master** and use the zoom tools at the top of the view area to zoom into the details, as you see in Figure 6.11:

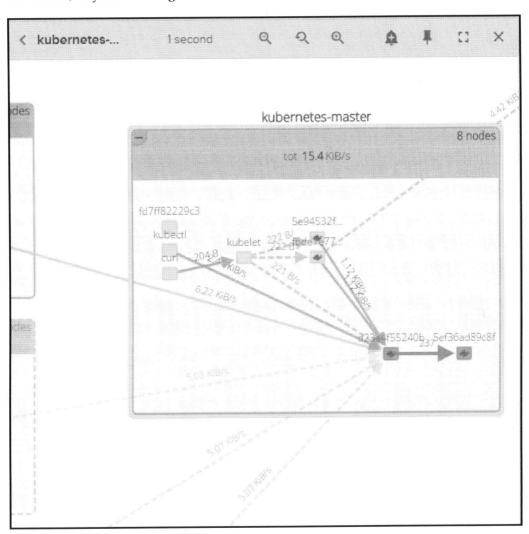

Figure 6.11. The Sysdig Cloud network topology detailed view

Note that we can now see all the components of Kubernetes running inside the master. We can see how the various components work together. We will see **kubectl** and the **kublet** process running, as well as a number of boxes with the Docker whale, which indicate that they are containers. If we zoom in and use the plus icon, we will see that these are the containers for core Kubernetes process, as we saw in the services running on the master section in *Chapter 1, Kubernetes and Container Operations.*

Also, if we pan over to the minion, we can also see **kublet**, which initiates communication, and follow it all the way through the `kube-apiserver` container in the master.

We can even see the instance probing for GCE metadata on **169.254.169.254**. This view is great in order to get a mental picture of how our infrastructure and underlying containers are talking to one another.

## Metrics

Next, let's switch over to the **Metrics** tab in the left-hand menu next to **Views**. Here, there are also a variety of helpful views.

Let's look at **capacity.estimated.request.total.count (avg)** under **System**. This view shows us an estimate of how many requests a node is capable of handling when fully loaded. This can be really useful for infrastructure planning.

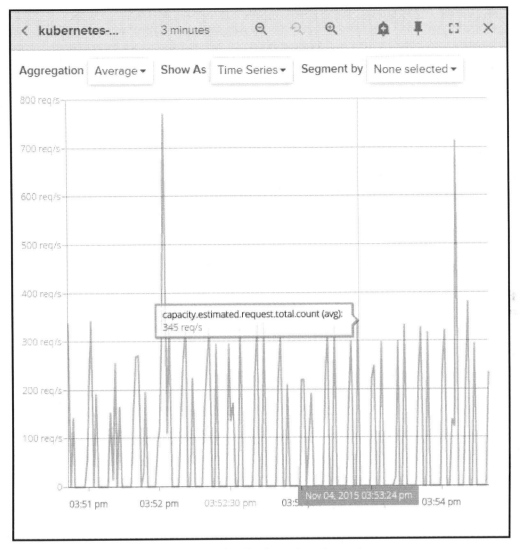

Figure 6.12. Sysdig Cloud capacity estimate view

# Alerting

Now that we have all this great information, let's create some notifications. Scroll back up to the top of the page and find the bell icon next to one of your minion entries. This will open a **New Alert** dialog. Here, we can set manual alerts similar to what we did earlier in the chapter. However, there is also the option to use **Baselines** and **Host comparison**.

Using the **Baseline** option is extremely helpful as Sysdig will watch the historical patterns of the node and alert us whenever one of the metrics strays outside the expected metric thresholds. No manual settings are required, so this can really save time for the notification setup and help our operations team to be proactive before issues arise. Refer to the following image:

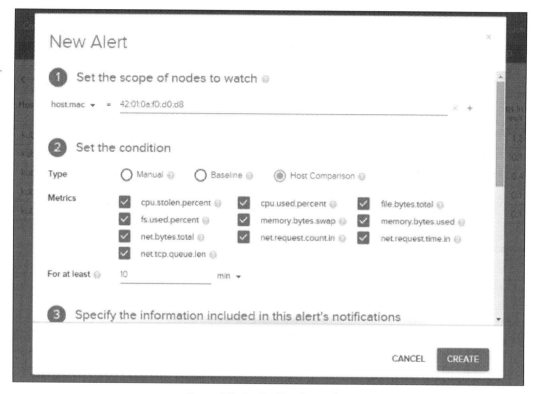

Figure 6.13. Sysdig Cloud new alert

The **Host Comparison** option is also a great help as it allows us to compare metrics with other hosts and alert whenever one host has a metric that differs significantly from the group. A great use case for this is monitoring resource usage across minion nodes to ensure that our scheduling constraints are not creating a bottleneck somewhere in the cluster.

You can choose whichever option you like, give it a name and description and choose a notification method. Sysdig supports e-mail, **SNS** (short for **Simple Notification Service**), and **PagerDuty** as notification methods. Once you have everything set, just click on **Create** and you will start to receive alerts as issues come up.

# Kubernetes support

An exciting new feature that has been recently released is support for integrating directly with the Kubernetes API. The agents make calls to K8s so that it is aware of metadata and the various constructs, such as pods and RCs.

We can check this out easily on the main dashboard by clicking the gear icon next to the word Show on the top bar. We should see some filter options as in the following figure (Figure 6.14). Click on the **Apply** button next to **Logical Apps Hierarchy - Kubernetes**. This will set a number of filters that organizes our list in order of namespace, RC, pods, and finally container ID.

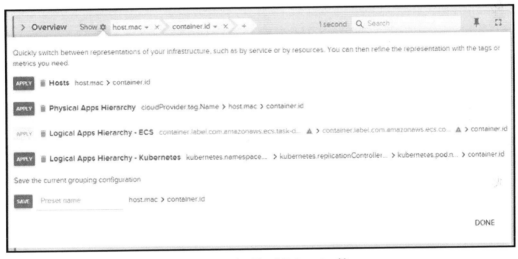

Figure 6.14. Sysdig Cloud Kubernetes filters

We can then select a default namespace from the list and use the detail views later, as we did before. By selecting the **Topology: Network Traffic** view, we can drill into the namespace and get a visual for each RC and the pods running within (see Figure 6.15):

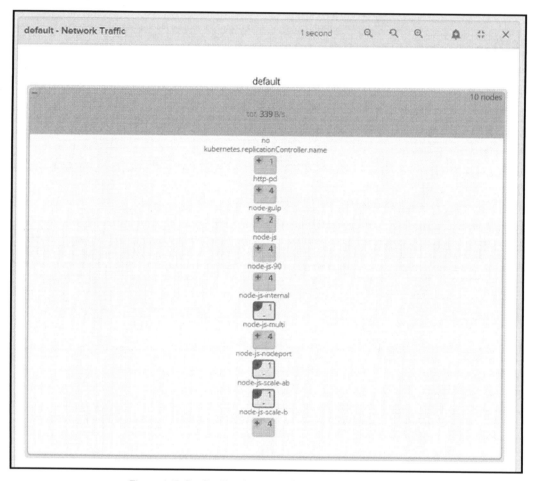

Figure 6.15. Sysdig Cloud Kubernetes-aware topology view

# The Sysdig command line

Whether you only use the open source tool or you are trying out the full Sysdig Cloud package, the command-line utility is a great companion to have to track down issues or get a deeper understanding of your system.

In the core tool, there is the main `sysdig` utility and also a command-line style UI named `csysdig`. Let's take a look at a few useful commands.

We'll need to SSH to the master or one of the minion nodes where we installed the Sysdig Cloud agents. It's a single command to install the CLI tools as follows:

```
$ curl -s https://s3.amazonaws.com/download.draios.com/stable/install-sysdig | sudo bash
```

 You can find instructions for other OSes at `http://www.sysdig.org/install/`.

First, we can see the process with the most network activity by issuing the following command:

```
$ sudo sysdig -pc -c topprocs_net
```

The following screenshot is the result of the preceding command:

| Bytes | Process | Host_pid | Container_pid | container.name |
|-------|---------|----------|---------------|----------------|
| 79.06KB | kube-apise | 5152 | 15 | host |
| 58.10KB | etcd | 5211 | 10 | host |
| 6.29KB | dragent | 19284 | 19292 | host |
| 4.52KB | kube-contr | 5164 | 11 | host |
| 4.11KB | etcd | 5211 | 11 | host |
| 1.95KB | kube-sched | 5227 | 13 | host |
| 1.72KB | sshd | 18963 | 18963 | host |

Figure 6.16. A Sysdig top process by network activity

This is an interactive view that will show us a top process in terms of network activity. Also, there are a plethora of commands to use with `sysdig`. A few other useful commands to try out include the following:

```
$ sudo sysdig -pc -c topprocs_cpu
```

```
$ sudo sysdig -pc -c topprocs_file
```

```
$ sudo sysdig -pc -c topprocs_cpu container.name=<Container Name NOT ID>
```

 More examples can be found at `http://www.sysdig.org/wiki/sysdig-examples/`.

# The csysdig command-line UI

Because we are in a shell on one of our nodes doesn't mean we can't have a UI. Csysdig is a customizable UI to explore all the metrics and insight that Sysdig provides. Simply type `csysdig` at the prompt:

```
$ csysdig
```

After entering csysdig, we see a real-time listing of all processes on the machine. At the bottom of the screen, you'll note a menu with various options. Click on **Views** or *F2* if you love to use your keyboard. On the left-hand menu, there are a variety of options, but we'll look at threads. Double-click to select **Threads**.

We can see all the threads currently running on the system and some information about the resource usage. By default, we see a big list that is updating often. If we click on the **Filter**, *F4* for the mouse challenged, we can slim down the list.

Type `kube-apiserver`, if you are on the master, or `kube-proxy`, if you are on a (minion) node, in the filter box and press enter. The view now filters for only the threads in that command.

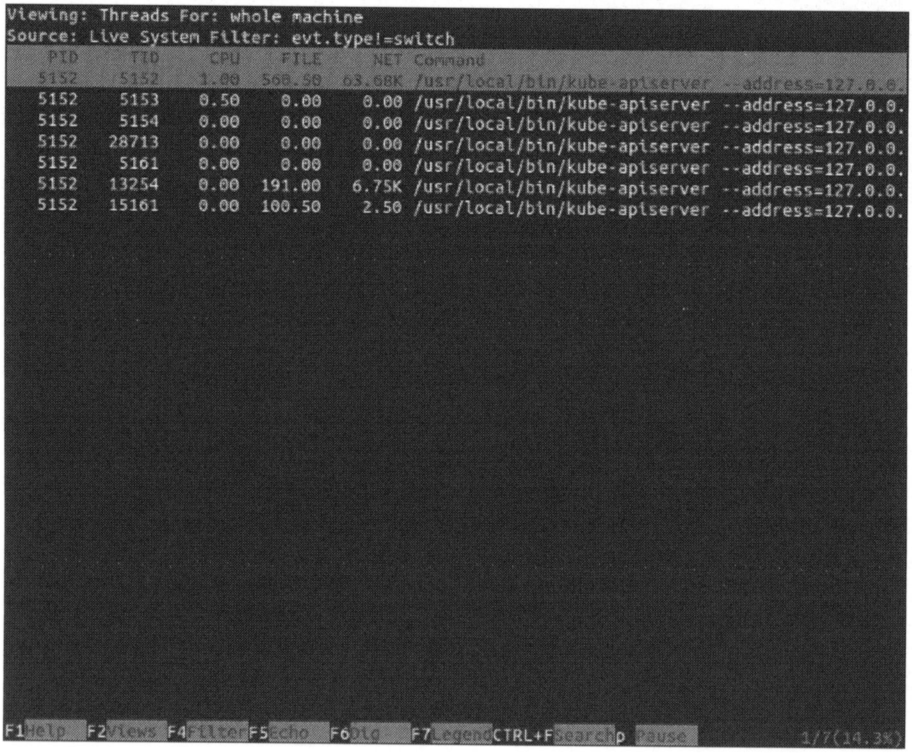

Figure 6.17. Csysdig threads

If we want to inspect a little further, we can simply select one of the threads in the list and click on **Dig** or *F6*. Now we see a detail listing of system calls from the command in real time. This can be a really useful tool to gain deep insight into the containers and processing running on our cluster.

Press **Back** or the *backspace* key to go back to the previous screen. Then, go to **Views** once more. This time, we will look at the **Containers** view. Once again, we can filter and also use the **Dig** view to get more in-depth visibility into what is happening at a system call level.

Another menu item you might note here is **Actions**, which is available in the newest release. These features allow us to go from process monitoring to action and response. It gives us the ability to perform a variety of actions from the various process views in csysdig. For example, the container view has actions to drop into a bash shell, kill containers, inspect logs, and more. It's worth getting to know the various actions and hotkeys and even add you own custom hotkeys for common operations.

# Summary

We took a quick look at monitoring and logging with Kubernetes. You should now be familiar with how Kubernetes uses cAdvisor and Heapster to collect metrics on all the resources in a given cluster. Furthermore, we saw how Kubernetes saves us time by providing InfluxDB and Grafana set up and configured out of the box. Dashboards are easily customizable for our everyday operational needs.

In addition, we looked at the built-in logging capabilities with FluentD and the Google Cloud Logging service. Also, Kubernetes gives us great time savings by setting up the basics for us.

Finally, you learned about the various third-party options available to monitor our containers and clusters. Using these tools will allow us to gain even more insight into the health and status of our applications. All these tools combine to give us a solid toolset to manage day-to-day operations.

# Footnotes

[1]`http://stackdriver.com/`

[2]`http://www.sysdig.org/wiki/`

# 7
# OCI, CNCF, CoreOS, and Tectonic

The first half of this chapter will cover how open standards encourage a diverse ecosystem of container implementations. We'll look at the Open Container Initiative and its mission to provide an open container specification as well. The second half of this chapter will cover CoreOS and its advantages as a host OS, including performance and support for various container implementations. Also, we'll take a brief look at the Tectonic enterprise offering from CoreOS.

This chapter will discuss the following topics:

- Why standards matter
- The Open Container Initiative and Cloud Native Computing Foundation
- Container specifications versus implementations
- CoreOS and its advantages
- Tectonic

## The importance of standards

Over the past two years, containerization technology has had a tremendous growth in popularity. While Docker has been at the center of this ecosystem, there is an increased number of players in the container space. There is already a number of alternatives to the containerization and Docker implementation itself (**rkt**, **Garden**, **LXD**, and so on). In addition, there is a rich ecosystem of third-party tools that enhance and compliment your container infrastructure. Kubernetes lands squarely on the orchestration side of this ecosystem, but the bottom line is that all these tools form the basis to build cloud native applications.

As we mentioned in the very beginning of the book, one of the most attractive things about containers is their ability to package our application for deployment across various environments (that is, development, testing, production) and various infrastructure providers (GCP, AWS, On-Premise, and so on).

To truly support this type of deployment agility, we need not only the container themselves to have a common platform, but also the underlying specifications to follow a common set of ground rules. This will allow for implementations that are both flexible and highly specialized. For example, some workloads may need to be run on a highly secure implementation. To provide this, the implementation will have to make more intentional decisions about some aspects of implementation. In either case, we will have more agility and freedom if our containers are built on some common structures that all implementations agree on and support.

# Open Container Initiative

One of the first initiatives to gain widespread industry engagement is the **Open Container Initiative (OCI)**. Among the industry collaborators are Docker, Red Hat, VMware, IBM, Google, AWS, and many more listed on the OCI website, that is, `https://www.opencontainers.org/`.

The purpose of the OCI is to split implementations, such as Docker and Rocket, from a standard specification for the format and runtime of containerized workloads. By their own terms, the goal of the OCI specification has three tenets[1]:

> *Creating a formal specification for container image formats and runtime, which will allow a compliant container to be portable across all major, compliant operating systems and platforms without artificial technical barriers.*

> *Accepting, maintaining and advancing the projects associated with these standards (the "Projects"). It will look to agree on a standard set of container actions (start, exec, pause,....) as well as runtime environment associated with container runtime.*

> *Harmonizing the above-referenced standard with other proposed standards, including the appc specification*

# Cloud Native Computing Foundation

A second initiative that also has a widespread industry acceptance is the **Cloud Native Computing Foundation** (**CNCF**). While still focused on containerized workloads, the CNCF operates a bit higher up the stack at an application design level. The purpose is to provide a standard set of tools and technologies to build, operate, and orchestrate cloud native application stacks. Cloud has given us access to a variety of new technologies and practices that can improve and evolve our classic software designs. This is also particularly focused at the new paradigm of microservice-oriented development.

As a founding participant in CNCF, Google has donated the Kubernetes open source project as the first step. The goal will be to increase interoperability in the ecosystem and support better integration with projects, starting off with Mesos.

 For more information on CNCF refer: `https://cncf.io/`

# Standard container specification

A core result of the OCI effort is the creation and development of the overarching container specification. The specification has five core principles for all containers to follow, which I will briefly paraphrase[2]:

- It must have **standard operations** to create, start, and stop containers across all implementations.

- It must be **content-agnostic**, which means that type of application inside the container does not alter the standard operation or publishing of the container itself.

- The container must be **infrastructure-agnostic** as well. Portability is paramount; therefore, the containers must be able to operate just as easily in GCE as in your company data center or on a developer's laptop.

- A container must also be **designed for automation**, which allows us to automate across the build, updating, and deployment pipelines. While this rule is a bit vague, the container implementation should not require onerous manual steps for creation and release.

- Finally, the implementation must support **industrial-grade delivery**. Once again, speaking to the build and deployment pipelines and requiring a streamlined efficiency to the portability and transit of the containers between infrastructure and deployment tiers.

The specification also defines core principles for container formats and runtimes. You can read more about the specifications on the GitHub project at:

```
https://github.com/opencontainers/specs
```

While the core specification can be a bit abstract, the **runC** implementation is a concrete example of the OCI specs in the form of a container runtime and image format. Also, you can read more of the technical details on GitHub at `https://github.com/opencontainers/runc`.

runC is the backing format and runtime for a variety of popular container tools. It was donated to OCI by Docker and was created from the same plumbing work used in the Docker platform. Since its release, it has had a welcome uptake by numerous projects.

Even the popular Open Source PaaS, **Cloud Founrdy** announced that it will use runC in Garden. Garden provides the containerization plumbing for Deigo, which acts as an orchestration layer similar to Kubernetes.

rkt was originally based on the **appc** specification. appc was actually an earlier attempt by the folks at CoreOS to form a common specification around containerization. Now that CoreOS is participating in OCI, they are working to help merge the appc specification into OCI; it should result in a higher level of compatibility across the container ecosystem.

# CoreOS

While the specifications provide us a common ground, there are also some trends evolving around the choice of OS for our containers. There are several tailor-fit OSes that are being developed specifically to run container workloads. Although implementations vary, they all have similar characteristics. Focus on a slim installation base, atomic OS updating, and signed applications for efficient and secure operations.

One OS that is gaining popularity is CoreOS. **CoreOS** offers major benefits for both security and resource utilization. It provides the later by removing package dependencies completely from picture. Instead, CoreOS runs all applications and services in containers. By providing only a small set of services required to support running containers and bypassing the need for hypervisor usage, CoreOS lets us use a larger portion of the resource pool to run our containerized applications. This allows users to gain higher performance from their infrastructure and better container to node (server) usage ratios.

**More container OSes**

There are several other container-optimized OSes that have emerged recently.

**Red Hat Enterprise Linux Atomic Host** focuses on security with **SELinux** enabled by default and "Atomic" updates to the OS similar to what we saw with CoreOS. Refer to the following link:

```
https://access.redhat.com/articles/rhel-atomic-
getting-started
```

**Ubuntu Snappy** also capitalizes on the efficiency and security gains of separating the OS components from the frameworks and applications. Using application images and verification signatures, we get an efficient Ubuntu-based OS for our container workloads:

```
http://www.ubuntu.com/cloud/tools/snappy
```

**VMware Photon** is another lightweight container OS that is optimized specifically for **vSphere** and the VMware platform. It runs Docker, rkt, and Garden and also has some experimental versions you can run on the popular public cloud offerings. Refer to the following link:

```
https://vmware.github.io/photon/
```

Using the isolated nature of containers, we increase reliability and decrease the complexity of updates for each application. Now applications can be updated along with supporting libraries whenever a new container release is ready.

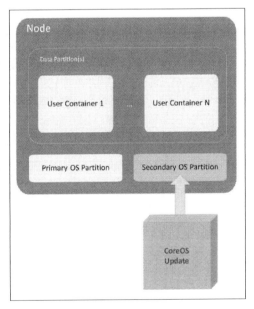

Figure 7.1. CoreOS updates

Finally, CoreOS has some added advantages in the realm of security. For starters, the OS can be updated as one whole unit instead of by individual packages (refer to Figure 7.1). This avoids many issues that arise from partial updates. To achieve this, CoreOS uses two partitions: one as the active OS partition and a secondary to receive a full update. Once updates are completed successfully, a reboot promotes the secondary partition. If anything goes wrong, the original partition is available for fail back.

The system owners can also control when those updates are applied. This gives us the flexibility to prioritize critical updates while working with real-world scheduling for the more common updates. In addition, the entire update is signed and transmitted via SSL for added security across the entire process.

# rkt

A central piece of the CoreOS ecosystem is its own container runtime, named rkt. As we mentioned earlier, rkt is another implementation with a specific focus on security. rkt's main advantage is in running the engine without a daemon as root the way Docker does today. Initially, rkt also had an advantage in establishing trust for container images. However, recent updates to Docker have made great strides with the new **Content Trust** feature.

The bottom line is that rkt is still an implementation focused on security to run containers in production. rkt does use an image format named **ACI**, but it also supports running Docker-based images. At the time of writing this book, it is only at version 0.11.0, but it's already gaining momentum as a way to run Docker images securely in production.

In addition, CoreOS recently announced integration with the **Intel® Virtualization Technology**, which allows containers to run in higher levels of isolation. This hardware-enhanced security allows the containers to be run inside a **Kernel-based Virtual Machine (KVM)** process providing isolation from the kernel similar to what we see with hypervisors today.

# etcd

Another central piece in the CoreOS ecosystem worth mentioning is their open source etcd project. etcd is a distributed and consistent key-value store. A RESTful API is used to interface with etcd, so it's easy to integrate with your project.

If it sounds familiar, it's because we saw this process running in *Chapter 1, Kubernetes and Container Operations,* under the *Services running on the master* section. Kubernetes actually utilizes etcd to keep track of cluster configuration and current state. K8s uses it for the service discovery capabilities as well.

# Kubernetes with CoreOS

Now that we understand the benefits, let's take a look at a Kubernetes cluster using CoreOS. The documentation supports a number of platforms, but one of the easiest to spin up is AWS with the CoreOS **CloudFormation** and CLI scripts.

 If you are interested in running Kubernetes with CoreOS on other platforms, you can find more details in the CoreOS documentation here:
`https://coreos.com/kubernetes/docs/latest/`

We can find the latest scripts for AWS here:

`https://github.com/coreos/coreos-kubernetes/releases/latest`

For this walk-through, we will use v0.1.0 (latest at the time of writing) of the scripts. We'll need a Linux machine with the AWS CLI installed and configured. See the *Working with other providers* section of *Chapter 1, Kubernetes and Container Operations*, for details on installing and configuring the AWS CLI. I recommend that you use a box with the Kubernetes control scripts already installed to avoid having to download `kubectl` separately.

Let's first download and extract the **tarball** from GitHub as follows:

```
$ wget https://github.com/coreos/coreos-kubernetes/releases/download/
v0.1.0/kube-aws-linux-amd64.tar.gz

$ tar xzvf kube-aws-linux-amd64.tar.gz
```

This will extract a single executable named `kube-aws`. This file will launch the AWS infrastructure in the same way that `kube-up.sh` did for us earlier.

Before we proceed, we need to create a key-pair to use on AWS. For this example, I create one key-pair named `kube-aws-key`. We can create a key in the console under the EC2 service on the left-hand menu and then select **Key Pairs**. Keys can also be created using the CLI.

Next, we will need to create a cluster definition file. In the same folder, we downloaded `kube-aws`; create a new file from the listing 7-1:

```
# Unique name of Kubernetes cluster. In order to deploy
# more than one cluster into the same AWS account, this
# name must not conflict with an existing cluster.
# clusterName: kubernetes

# Name of the SSH keypair already loaded into the AWS
# account being used to deploy this cluster.
```

```
keyName: kube-aws-key

# Region to provision Kubernetes cluster
region: us-east-1

# Availability Zone to provision Kubernetes cluster
#availabilityZone:

# DNS name routable to the Kubernetes controller nodes
# from worker nodes and external clients. The deployer
# is responsible for making this name routable
externalDNSName: kube-aws
# Number of worker nodes to create
#workerCount: 1


# Location of kube-aws artifacts used to deploy a new
# Kubernetes cluster. The necessary artifacts are already
# available in a public S3 bucket matching the version
# of the kube-aws tool. This parameter is typically
# overwritten only for development purposes.
#artifactURL: https://coreos-kubernetes.s3.amazonaws.com/<VERSION>
```

*Listing 7-1*: `coreos-cluster.yaml`

We have a few things to note. We have `keyName` set to the key we just created, `kube-aws-key`. The region is set to `us-east-1` (Northern Virginia), so edit this if you prefer a different region. In addition, `clustername` and `workerCount` are commented out, but their defaults are as listed, `kubernetes` and `1`, respectively. `workerCount` defines the number of slaves, so you can increase this value if you need more.

In addition, we have a placeholder DNS entry. The value for `externalDNSName` is set to `kube-aws`.

> For simplicity's sake, we can simply add an entry for `kube-aws` in the `/etc/hosts` file. For a production system, we would want a real entry that we could expose through Route 53, another DNS registrar, or a local DNS entry.

Now we can spin up the CoreOS cluster:

```
$ ./kube-aws up --config="coreos-cluster.yaml"
```

We should get the master IP in the console output under controller IP. We will need to update the IP address for `kube-aws` in our `/etc/hosts` file or DNS provider. We can also get the master IP by checking our running instances in AWS. It should be labeled `kube-aws-controller`.

```
$ vi /etc/hosts
```

There you have it! We now have a cluster running CoreOS. The script creates all the necessary AWS resources, such as **Virtual Private Clouds (VPCs)**, security groups, and IAM role.

> Note that if this is a fresh box, you will need to download `kubectl` separately as it is not bundled with `kube-aws`:
>
> `wget https://storage.googleapis.com/kubernetes-release/release/v1.0.6/bin/linux/amd64/kubectl`

We can now use `kubectl` to see our new cluster:

```
$ kubectl --kubeconfig=clusters/kubernetes/kubeconfig get nodes
```

We should see a single node listed with the EC2 internal DNS as the name. Note `kubeconfig`, this tells Kubernetes to use the configuration file for the cluster we just created instead of the previous GCE cluster we have been working thus far. This is useful if we want to manage multiple clusters from the same machine.

# Tectonic

Running Kubernetes on CoreOS is a great start, but you may find that you want a higher level of support. Enter **Tectonic**, the CoreOS enterprise offering for running Kubernetes with CoreOS. Tectonic uses many of the components we've already discussed. CoreOS is the OS and both Docker and rkt runtimes are supported. In addition, Kubernetes, etcd, and flannel are packaged together to give a full stack of cluster orchestration. We discussed flannel briefly in *Chapter 3, Core Concepts – Networking, Storage, and Advanced Services*. It is an overlay network that uses a model similar to the native Kubernetes model, and it uses etcd as a backend.

Offering a support package similar to Red Hat, CoreOS are also providing 24x7 support for the open source software that Tectonic is built on. Tectonic also provides regular cluster updates and a nice dashboard with views for all the components of Kubernetes. **CoreUpdate** allows users to have more control of the automatic updates. In addition, it ships with **Tectonic Identity** for SSO across the cluster and the **Quay Enterprise**, which provides a secure container registry behind your own firewall.

# Dashboard highlights

Here are some highlights of the Tectonic dashboard:

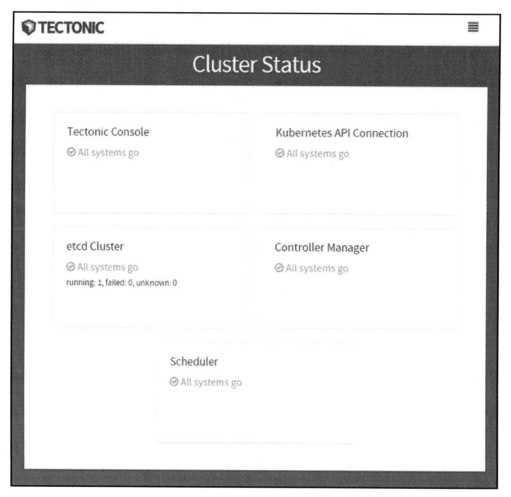

Figure 7.2. The Tectonic main dashboard

Tectonic is now generally available and the dashboard already has some nice features. As you can see in Figure 7.3, we can see a lot of detail about our replication controller and can even use the GUI to scale up and down with the click of a button:

**TECTONIC**   Services   Replication Controllers   Pods   Nodes   More ▾        My Account ⚙

← Back to Replication Controllers                    node-js

## Desired State

**Replicas:**        ⊟   [ 3 ]   ⊕

**Controller Labels:**   [ deployement=demo ×   name=node-js ×   app=frontend ]
                         Labels for this controller.

**Label Query:**        [ deployment=demo ×   name=node-js ×   app=frontend ]
                        Write a label query that will match labels on new or existing pods.

## Desired Pod State

These containers make up a pod. All of these containers are deployed together onto nodes in the cluster.

**Pod Labels:**        [ deployment=demo ×   name=node-js ×   app=frontend ]
                       Each pod instance will have these labels. Services matching these labels will automatically send traffic to containers.

**Pod Volumes:**       0 Volumes ›
                       Named volumes that may be accessed by any containers in the pod.

## Containers

[ Add Another Container ]

                                                                              ⊗

CONTAINER NAME             CONTAINER IMAGE                    CONTAINER VERSION/TAG
[ node-js ]                [ jonbaier/node-express-info ]     [ latest ]

VOLUMES                    PRIMARY COMMAND                    PULL POLICY
0 Volume Mounts ›          Default Command ›                  Always Pull ›

PORTS                      LIFECYCLE HOOKS                    LIVENESS PROBE
1 Ports ›                  Not Configured ›                   Not Configured ›

ENVIRONMENT                                                   RESOURCE LIMITS
0 Variables ›                                                 Not Configured ›

[ Update Desired State ]   Cancel

📄 Documentation    💬 IRC #coreos

Figure 7.3. Tectonic replication controller detail

Another nice feature is the **Streaming events** page. Here, we can watch the events live, pause, and filter based on event severity and resource type.

Figure 7.4. Events stream

A useful feature to browse anywhere in the dashboard system is the namespace filtering option. Simply click on the gear in the top-right corner of the page, and we can filter our views by namespace. This can be helpful if we want to filter out the Kubernetes system pods or just look at a particular collection of resources.

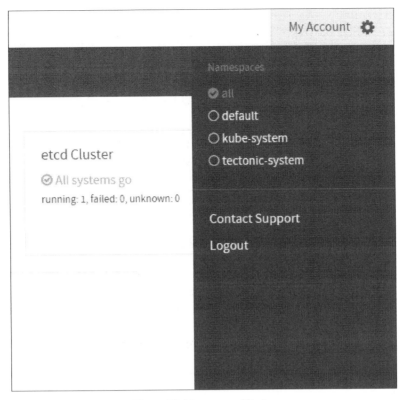

Figure 7.5. Namespace filtering

# Summary

In this chapter, we looked at the emerging standards bodies in the container community and how they are shaping the technology for the better with open specifications. We also took a closer look at CoreOS, a key player in both the container and Kubernetes community. We explored the technology they are developing to enhance and compliment container orchestration and saw first-hand how to use some of it with Kubernetes. Finally, we looked at the supported enterprise offering of Tectonic and some of the features that will be available soon.

# Footnotes

[1] `https://www.opencontainers.org/faq/` (#11 on the page)

[2] `https://github.com/opencontainers/specs/blob/master/principles.md`

# 8
# Towards Production-Ready

In this chapter, we'll look at considerations to move to production. We will also show some helpful tools and third-party projects available in the Kubernetes community at large and where you can go to get more help.

This chapter will discuss the following topics:

- Production characteristics
- The Kubernetes ecosystem
- Where to get help

## Ready for production

We've walked through a number of typical operations using Kubernetes. As we saw, K8s offers a variety of features and abstractions that ease the burden of day-to-day management for container deployments.

There are many characteristics that define a production-ready system for containers. Figure 8.1 provides a high-level view of the major concerns for production-ready clusters. This is by no means an exhaustive list, but it's meant to provide some solid ground heading into production operations.

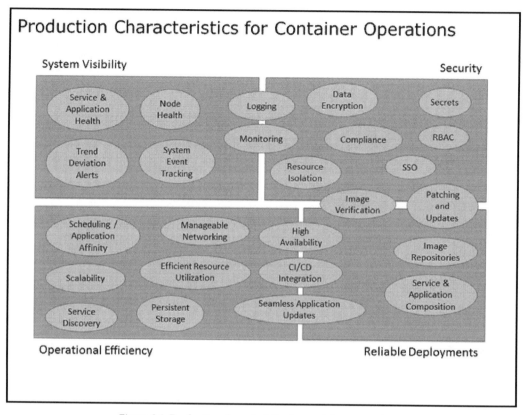

Figure 8.1. Production characteristics for container operations.

We saw how the core concepts and abstractions of Kubernetes address a few of these concerns. The service abstraction has built in service discovery and health checking at both the service and application level. We also get seamless application updates and scalability from the replication controller construct. All three core abstractions of services, replication controllers, and pods work with a core scheduling and affinity ruleset and give us easy service and application composition.

There is a built-in support for a variety of persistent storage options, and the networking model provides manageable network operations with options to work with other third-party providers. Also, we took a brief look at CI/CD integration with some of the popular tools in the marketplace.

Furthermore, we have built-in system events tracking, and with the major cloud providers, an out-of-the box setup for monitoring and logging. We also saw how this can be extended with third-party providers such as StackDriver and Sysdig. These services also address overall node health and proactive trend deviation alerts.

The core constructs also help us address high availability in our application and service layers. The scheduler can be used with autoscaling mechanisms to provide this at a node level. There is also a support to make the Kubernetes master itself highly available.

We finally explored a new breed of operating systems that give us a slim base to build on and secure update mechanisms for patching and updates. The slim base, together with scheduling, can help us with efficient resource utilization. In addition, there is functionality in the OS and Docker itself for trusted image verification.

# Security

We have not explored many of the areas around security in depth. The subject itself could fill its own book. However, Kubernetes does provide one very important construct out of the box named **secrets**.

Secrets give us a way to store sensitive information without including plaintext versions in our resource definition files. Secrets can be mounted to the pods that need them and then accessed within the pod as files with the secret values as content.

Secrets are still in their early stages, but a vital component for production operations. There are several improvements planned here for future releases.

To learn more about secrets and even get a walk-through, check out the **Secrets** section in the K8s user guide at `http://kubernetes.io/v1.0/docs/user-guide/secrets.html`.

# Ready, set, go

While there are still some gaps, a variety of the remaining security and operations concerns are actively being addresses by third-party companies as we will see in the following section. Going forward, the Kubernetes project will continue to evolve, and the community of projects and partners around K8s and Docker will also grow. The community is closing the remaining gaps at a phenomenal pace.

# Third-party companies

Since the Kubernetes project's initial release, there has been a growing ecosystem of partners. We looked at CoreOS in the previous chapter, but there are many more projects and companies in this space. We will highlight a few that may be useful as you move towards production.

# Private registries

In many situations, organizations will not want to place their applications and/or intellectual property in public repositories. For those cases, a private registry solution is helpful in securely integrating deployments end to end.

Google Cloud offers the **Google Container Registry**: `https://cloud.google.com/container-registry/`.

Docker has their own **Trusted Registry** offering: `https://www.docker.com/docker-trusted-registry`.

**Quay.io** also provides secure private registries, vulnerability scanning, and comes from the CoreOS team: `https://quay.io/`.

# Google Container Engine

Google was the main author of the original Kubernetes project and still a major contributor. Although this book has mostly focused on running Kubernetes on our own, Google is also offering a fully managed container service through the Google Cloud Platform.

 Find more information on the **Google Container Engine** (**GKE**) website: `https://cloud.google.com/container-engine/`

Kubernetes will be installed on GCE and managed by Google engineers. They also provide private registries and integration with your existing private networks.

**Create your first GKE cluster**

From the GCP console, under **Compute**, click on **Container Engine** and then **Container Clusters**.

If this is your first time creating a cluster, you'll have an information box in the middle of the page. Click on the **Create a container cluster** button.

Choose a name for your cluster and the zone. You'll also be able to choose the machine type (instance size) for your nodes and how many nodes (cluster size) you want in your cluster. The master is managed and updated by the Google team themselves. Leave the **Cloud Logging** checked. Click on **Create**, and in a few minutes, you'll have a new cluster ready for use.

You'll need kubectl that is included with the Google SDK to begin using your GKE cluster. Refer to *Chapter 1, Kubernetes and Container Operations,* for details on installing the SDK. Once we have the SDK, we can configure kubectl and the SDK for our cluster using the steps outlined at https://cloud.google.com/container-engine/docs/before-you-begin#install_kubectl.

# Twistlock

**Twistlock.io** is a vulnerability and hardening tool tailor-made for containers. They provide the ability to enforce policy and audit risk at the container level itself. While not specifically designed for Kubernetes, this promises to be a core piece of governance and compliance for container operations. Here is a brief description from their website:

*"Twistlock is the first security solution designed specifically to protect containerized computing and micro-services.*

*The Twistlock Security Suite detects vulnerabilities, hardens container images, and enforces security policies across the lifecycle of applications.*

*We are portable and agentless; we run everywhere your containers do... dev workstations, public clouds, private clouds."*

Please refer to the Twistlock website for more information: https://www.twistlock.io/

# Kismatic

**Kismatic** was founded by a few folks with ties to both the Kubernetes and the Mesos ecosystems. They are aiming to provide enterprise support for Kubernetes. They were early contributors and built much of the user interface we saw in *Chapter 1, Kubernetes and Container Operations*. In addition, they are building the following plugins, as listed on their site.

> *"Role-based access controls (RBAC): Cluster-level virtualization is achieved using Kubernetes namespaces, a mechanism in Kubernetes for partitioning resources created by users into a logically named group. We extend Kubernetes namespaces with support for RBAC, the standard enterprise systems security method used to implement mandatory access control (MAC) or discretionary access control (DAC).*
>
> *Kerberos for bedrock authentication: Kubernetes currently uses client certificates, tokens, or HTTP basic authentication to authenticate users for API calls. For many enterprises, this level of authentication fails to meet production demands. Kismatic extends existing functionality by taking the API server tokens issued after the user has been (re)authenticated and integrating with bedrock authentication in Kerberos.*
>
> *LDAP/AD integration: For enterprises looking to manage user access via existing directory services, Kismatic integrates Kubernetes such services for authentication through LDAP / Active Directory.*
>
> *Auditing controls: In compliance sensitive enterprise environments, we have recognized that rich auditing and logging instrumentation and persistence are key to production stability. Therefore, we are excited to announce our audit log plugin for Kubernetes, providing a trusted way to track security-relevant information on your running Kubernetes microservices and cluster activities."*

 Please refer to the following Kismatic website for more information: `https://kismatic.com/`

# Mesosphere (Kubernetes on Mesos)

**Mesosphere** itself is building a commercially supported product (**DCOS**) around the open source Apache Mesos project. **Apache Mesos** is a cluster management system that offers scheduling and resource sharing a bit like Kubernetes itself, but at a much higher level. The open source project is used by several well-known companies, such as **Twitter** and **AirBnB**.

Get more information on the Mesos OS project and the Mesosphere offerings at these sites:

- `http://mesos.apache.org/`
- `https://mesosphere.com/`

Mesos by its nature is modular and allows the use of different frameworks for a variety of platforms. A Kubernetes framework is now available, so we can take advantage of the cluster managing in Mesos while still maintaining the useful application-level abstractions in K8s. Refer to the following link:

`https://github.com/mesosphere/kubernetes-mesos`

# Deis

The **Deis** project provides an open source **Platform as a Service (PaaS)** solution. This allows companies to deploy their own PaaS on premise or in the public cloud. Deis uses CoreOS as an underlying operating system and runs applications in Docker. Version 1.9 now has the preview support for Kubernetes as a scheduler. While this is not production-ready at the moment, it's a good one to watch if you are interested in deploying your own PaaS.

You can refer to the following website for more information on Deis:
`http://docs.deis.io/en/latest/customizing_deis/`
`choosing-a-scheduler/#k8s-scheduler`

# OpenShift

Another PaaS solution is **OpenShift** from Red Hat. The OpenShift platform uses the Red Hat Atomic platform as a secure and slim OS for running containers. In version 3, Kubernetes has been added as the orchestration layer for all container operations on your PaaS. This is great combination to manage PaaS installations at a large scale.

More information on OpenShift can be found here:
`https://enterprise.openshift.com/`

# Where to learn more

The Kubernetes project is an open source effort, so there is a broad community of contributors and enthusiasts. One great resource in order to find more assistance is the Kubernetes **Slack** channel as follows:

```
http://slack.kubernetes.io/
```

There is also a containers group on Google groups. You can join here:

```
https://groups.google.com/forum/#!forum/google-containers
```

If you enjoyed this book, you can find more of my articles, how tos, and various musings on my blogs and twitter page as follows:

- `http://www.cloudtp.com/meet-the-advisors/jonathan-baier/`
- `https://medium.com/@grizzbaier`
- `https://twitter.com/grizzbaier`

# Summary

In this final chapter, we left a few breadcrumbs to guide you on your continued journey with Kubernetes. You should have a solid set of production characteristics to get you started. There is a wide community in both the Docker and Kubernetes world. There are also a few additional resources we provided if you need a friendly face along the way.

By now, we have seen the full spectrum of container operations with Kubernetes. You should be more confident in how Kubernetes can streamline the management of your container deployments and how you can plan to move containers off the developer laptops and onto production servers.

# Index

## Thank you for buying
# Getting Started with Kubernetes

## About Packt Publishing

Packt, pronounced 'packed', published its first book, *Mastering phpMyAdmin for Effective MySQL Management*, in April 2004, and subsequently continued to specialize in publishing highly focused books on specific technologies and solutions.

Our books and publications share the experiences of your fellow IT professionals in adapting and customizing today's systems, applications, and frameworks. Our solution-based books give you the knowledge and power to customize the software and technologies you're using to get the job done. Packt books are more specific and less general than the IT books you have seen in the past. Our unique business model allows us to bring you more focused information, giving you more of what you need to know, and less of what you don't.

Packt is a modern yet unique publishing company that focuses on producing quality, cutting-edge books for communities of developers, administrators, and newbies alike. For more information, please visit our website at www.packtpub.com.

## About Packt Open Source

In 2010, Packt launched two new brands, Packt Open Source and Packt Enterprise, in order to continue its focus on specialization. This book is part of the Packt Open Source brand, home to books published on software built around open source licenses, and offering information to anybody from advanced developers to budding web designers. The Open Source brand also runs Packt's Open Source Royalty Scheme, by which Packt gives a royalty to each open source project about whose software a book is sold.

## Writing for Packt

We welcome all inquiries from people who are interested in authoring. Book proposals should be sent to author@packtpub.com. If your book idea is still at an early stage and you would like to discuss it first before writing a formal book proposal, then please contact us; one of our commissioning editors will get in touch with you.

We're not just looking for published authors; if you have strong technical skills but no writing experience, our experienced editors can help you develop a writing career, or simply get some additional reward for your expertise.

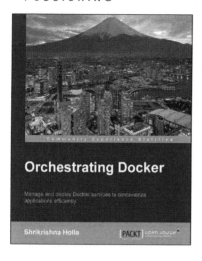

## CoreOS Essentials

ISBN: 978-1-78528-394-9          Paperback: 132 pages

Develop effective computing networks to deploy your applications and servers using CoreOS

1. Get to grips with the basics of CoreOS valong with managing clusters.

2. Write and deploy systemd and fleet units to launch Docker containers.

3. A comprehensive, easy-to-follow guide with an introduction to the new Rocket App Container and the Google Kubernetes cluster manager.

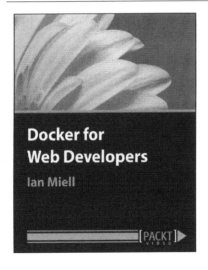

## Docker for Web Developers [Video]

ISBN: 978-1-78439-067-9          Duration: 1:31 hours

Accelerate your web development skills on real web projects in record time with Docker

1. Supercharge your web development process while ensuring that everything works smoothly.

2. Win at 2048 using Docker's commit and restore functionality.

3. Use the Docker Hub workflow to automate the rebuilding of your web projects.

4. Full of realistic examples, this is a step-by-step journey to becoming a Docker expert!.

Please check **www.PacktPub.com** for information on our titles

Made in the USA
San Bernardino, CA
25 May 2017